A Nightingale Sang

Published by Rosbeg Books
Westport, Ireland

ISBN-13: 978-1482625264
ISBN-10: 1482625261

First Edition: March 2013
Printed in the United States of America

Prologue

3rd September 1939

The Irish Mail disgorged its
*   overload of Irish Guards and me*
because today there's going to be a war.

We're going to Danzig, they're singing
You're going to die, I think
*   And I'm crying.*

A Nightingale Sang

Chapter 1

1939

It was a glorious morning in London. The only signs of imminent war were the fat silver barrage balloons floating in the cloudless sky. The streets were deserted. Everyone was at home waiting for the dreaded news. A declaration of war was inevitable now.

Summer had come early in 1939. The good weather at Easter lasted well into June. The Spanish Civil War had ended in victory for Franco. King Zog and Queen Geraldine, with their three-day old baby, had been thrown out of Albania. Europe was changing, but there was a whole new world to be explored now that schooldays were over. War would put an end to all our hopes and plans, so we chose to ignore the warning signs.

There had been a temporary break in the good weather, but by the middle of August the sun shone again and I decided to take my holiday in Ireland.

In Rosbeg we woke up every morning to cloudless skies and blue seas; and Clew Bay with its hundreds of islands looked heavenly. It was no trouble to ignore the uneasiness on the continent, where there were rumours of

Hitler's intention to take over the Polish port of Danzig to give Germany a corridor to the North Sea.

On one of my last days at home, we drove to Achill Island. We stood on the cliff above Keem Bay dazzled in the turquoise sea rolling up the beach below. That magic day was to become a treasured memory that would often cheer me in the dark days to come, because by then there was little doubt that we were to be faced with a major conflict.

German troops, who had already invaded Austria and Czechoslovakia, had crossed the Polish border on the 1st September. The Poles were putting up a valiant fight against numerically superior forces, but already there was every sign that the struggle would be in vain and could not be ignored by the western powers.

On the 2nd September, my lifelong friend Nan and I returned to London. The small country stations were deserted and eerily silent as the train rattled on its way to Dublin. It seemed the whole world was holding its breath.

We took a taxi from the Broadstone Station in Dublin to Dun Laoghaire and there the scene was totally different. Hundreds of men with kitbags were converging on the mail boat. There wasn't a woman in sight. There was a lot of excitement and men calling out to each other as though they hadn't met for a long time. Two of the men joined us.

"Give us your bag, love," one of them said to me. "What

are you doing here at a time like this? You should be at home, or are you going home?"

"No, I'm at college in London."

"Well, you'd be better off in Ireland. There's going to be a war, you know. All this lot are Irish Guard Reserves. We've been called up and we're expecting to be sent to Danzig on Monday. They can't let Poland down the way they sold out Czechoslovakia."

"I agree that appeasement hasn't worked," I said.

"I'll get you a seat," he said as we walked up the gangway. "We'll keep an eye on you. You'll be safe as houses. This lot are alright, though some of them look at bit rough," and he laughed.

"I'm not worried honestly, but I suppose there'll be a blackout in England tonight. I don't fancy that."

"You haven't a thing to worry about while we're around. Here you are now," he said, choosing a seat in the corner. "We won't be moving far from the bar."

"Thank you," I said. "I appreciate your help."

He seemed to think that was funny, and maybe it did sound a bit stilted. It was sometimes awkward being young.

The place was jam-packed. On deck I had seen two women with yellow hair and hard faces, but there was no sign of them now; only men everywhere. There was a lot of noise, from the engines as well as the excited voices of men on a mission. I was shocked into silence by the awful reality of the situation. I took my book out.

I was reading 'Gone with the Wind', the story of another terrible war in defence of a way of life that was already an anachronism. At least we hoped this war would be justified, but how much would it change our lives.

The noise was becoming louder and I began to feel uneasy. There was an argument.

"The bloody Pope hasn't done much to stop the atrocities against the Jews anyway." This came from a fresh-faced young man who was obviously not of the company. It was followed by a stunned silence. They were all looking at him and I held my breath. Were they going to fight?

A giant of a man, the worse for drink, bore down on him. "Say that again," he said.

"Take it easy," someone said. "You'll frighten the wee girls."

"You watch your tongue," the giant hissed at the young fellow, who beat a hasty retreat. We breathed a sigh of relief and went back to our books.

'Gone with the Wind' was very much alive for me. On another holiday I had stood among the ghosts on the battlefield at Gettysburg, where the fate of the southern States was sealed in the bitter winter of 1863. I could imagine the proud southerners marching up the valley of the Shenandoah River under the command of General Robert E. Lee, and their desolation when they were left at the end of the day to bury their six thousand dead.

Chapter 1 - 1939

It would be another two years before Lee, in full-dress uniform, surrendered to General Ulysses S. Grant. The alcoholic Grant, who hated the war that separated him from his beloved wife, was wearing the blue short of a private; but Lee had buried his high hopes with the dead at Gettysburg.

The kindly Echo, who had left us her voice when she had died, reminded me of Abraham Lincoln's immortal words in that haunted place. "That the dead will not be forgotten and that the Government of the people, for the people and by the people, will not perish from the earth." Isn't that why we're facing another war, I thought.

The guardsman interrupted my reverie. He brought a glass of lemonade. "How's it going?" he enquired.
"Fine, and thank you for this," I said.
"You appreciate it." He was teasing and I was embarrassed. "They call me Joe," he said then.
"And I'm Frances Carolan and this is my friend Nan."
"I'm pleased to meet you Frances Carolan," he said.
"You too Nan," and we both laughed. I liked Joe.

Someone was singing now, a pleasant tenor voice and there was silence for the song.

Though the last glimpse of Erin with sorrow I see
Yet wherever thou art shall seem Erin to me.

All their words are merry and all their songs are sad, I thought, and I felt sad too. What lay ahead for these 'splendid soldiers' as General Sir Brian Horrocks would describe the

Irish Guards? Indeed, what lay ahead for any of us? How many of us would survive the war?

When we got to Holyhead, Joe came to carry the case again. We walked the length of the train looking for some empty seats, but there weren't any, so we joined the scores of men who were sitting in the corridors. They were all pretty drunk and becoming maudlin. 'Mother Macree' and 'Erin go Brágh' were going to get the works on the way to London.

At Crewe Joe got out at the blacked out station and brought back two mugs of tea. It looked lonely out there – quiet and lonely. I had been travelling this way for five years now and Crewe was always bustling and filled with light. Now, apart from the dim light over the tea stall, there was gloom. It was ghostly.

I had never drunk tea in my life, but I was going to finish this if it killed me. I couldn't believe how awful it was. It looked like tar, I thought, but I drank it and thanked him again.

After Crewe, the soldier went to sleep and soon his head was resting on my shoulder. I was afraid to move, so I leant my face against his hair and slept for a while as well.

In the cold dawn, as we were approaching Euston, he woke up and looked at me in surprise. It made me laugh.
"You're a nice kid," he said, and he kissed me. "Look after yourself."
"You too," I said.
"Where are you going now?"

"I'm going to leave my case in the Left Luggage and go and look for a church."

"I'd like to come with you," he said. "We'll be needing all of the prayers we can get."

'You'll always know a catholic church,' my mother had once said. 'Because there'll be a sanctuary lamp in front of the altar.' Well we found one with a sanctuary lamp, but the vicar came and told us it was not Roman and directed us to another one. I guessed he had to do this all of the time, and we obviously looked as though we'd been up all night. We said that we'd like to stay.

"We want to pray that there won't be a war," I said.

"Oh they can't do that," said Joe. "We're going to Danzig on Monday anyway."

Afterwards, we parted company and travelled in different directions towards an uncertain future. I took a taxi to the YWCA in Regents Park. Now only God knew what would happen to any of us.

The guardsmen went on to their barracks. In the years that followed, I would wonder now and again how many of the men who had filled the Irish Mail train on the eve of the war had survived. They always seemed to be in the thick of the fighting, and I would offer a silent prayer sometimes for Joe, who took such good care of me when the world was about to be turned upside down.

A Nightingale Sang

Chapter 2

1939

The taxi driver wanted to talk on our way to Regents Park.

"Eleven o'clock they'll be telling us the worst," he said. "Have you just arrived?"

"No, I was on the Irish Mail earlier."

"That was crowded, wasn't it?" he said. I thought they'd all be stopping at home seein' as they're not goin' to join us."

"The train was full of Irish Guard Reserves coming over to fight with the British Army," I said.

He grunted. "Where did you say you wanted to go?"

"To Regents Park - the YWCA."

He drove around by the Nash Terraces. It all looked so elegant and peaceful. Hadn't it been like that forever? Here was the capital city of a mighty empire. Surely nothing could change it now. In spite of the sunshine, I suddenly felt cold. The driver had upset me. Was I crazy to leave home?

When I got to the club, the girls were standing round the radio in the big sitting room. They were waiting for the momentous announcement. Cynthia waved and Lyn came and put her arm around me. "You've heard?" I nodded. "We're waiting for Chamberlain," she said.

"This is the BBC Home and Overseas Service ..." and then Mr. Chamberlain's voice, softer than usual, was telling us of asking for an undertaking from Herr Hitler that he would withdraw his troops from Poland. "No such undertaking has been received and this country is now at war with Germany."

"This country is now at war with Germany." There was silence. Everyone was alone with their fears and speculations. Some looked as though they were praying. What would become of us?

The world we had known was coming to an end.

"This country is now at war with Germany." The words were making a record in my ear. I could hear them above the blood hammering in my eardrums. No one broke the long silence. How many of us had harboured a hope that there would be a last-minute reprieve? I, for one, had hoped for a miracle, but now we knew the worst. We were facing a dark tunnel into the unknown.

Mrs. Hunt, who was in charge, came in. She had hurried back from a service in the Guards' Chapel at Wellington Barracks, which became a favourite place to worship during the war. She was anxious to reassure us of the safety of the building.

"The basement has been reinforced," she said, "and there are bunks down there for everyone. That's where we'll go when the air raid warnings are sounded. I went through the last war when there were twenty-seven air raids on London.

We survived that, and we'll get through this one safely together."

We were grateful for her reassurance. We all knew the last war was hell for the men in the trenches, but we felt that civilians had got off comparatively lightly in England. It was not what anyone expected this time.

We thought there would be air raids from day one, and the first alarm, fifteen minutes after war was declared, sent us rushing to the basement and, with cook still carrying her gravy ladle, we waited for Armageddon.

Maybe an enemy plane had crossed the cliffs of Dover, but no bombs were dropped, no black crosses desecrated the winged fighters over the capital and, after fifteen minutes or so, we crawled out of our burrow and decided that war might not be so frightening after all.

It was not until the following morning we heard that the war at sea had already started. Hitler had evidently decided that England's survival depended on her imports. How could she conduct a war without oil? How could she feed and clothe the large population that overcrowded her limited space without imported food and fabrics? It would be impossible. Her ships must be destroyed. Britain, isolated from her main suppliers, would soon be defeated and, from the first day until the European war ended in May 1945, there were daily attacks on shipping.

The Liner *Athenia* was torpedoed and sunk and, over the following months and years, thousands of men and countless thousands of tons of shipping went to the bottom of the ocean. There seemed to be no way of stopping the U-boats, and the escorts were often totally inadequate against the wolf packs. That was how the U-boats operated, in packs lying in wait for their quarry and, from their point of view, it worked very well.

Lyn suggested that she should come with me after lunch. "You will have to collect a gas mask, ration book, clothing coupons and an identity card."

Although it was Sunday, the office was open and there were long queues. I collected everything I needed. At the stroke of a pen I had become YASA 794985 and, being Irish, I would have to report regularly.

At college in the morning, it seemed that half the people I'd known had gone already. I felt sorry for the young men who had no choice. "This bloody war," they were saying, their hopes and plans shattered at eighteen years old.

At least my friend Tom Faulkener was there, for the time being anyway. It was Tom who had introduced me to opera at Covent Garden when I first arrived. He would go up to the city at crack of dawn to queue for the tickets we wanted. It meant paying sixpence for a little stool to sit in the queue until the box office opened. Covent Garden had an enthusiastic following of young people who had very little money.

Chapter 2 - 1939

Tom would walk on the Downs with me at the weekend and he was always there to encourage my efforts at the local ice rink. Everything was more fun because Tom was there, so I could hardly believe my ears when he told me he had volunteered for the Marines, although he was not yet eighteen. The Marines were tough, I thought, not like Tom.

"Why've you done that?" I asked him.
"I didn't want to wait for the call-up. They might put me in the infantry. I'd hate that."

The world had turned upside down. I was sad. We'd been arranging dances for the Jewish refugees from Hitler's regime and we knew all about its cruelty, but I'd had German friends at school and I thought a lot about them. My particular friend had just joined the Auxiliary Territorial Service, the women's branch of the army, but she would never rise above the rank of private because her mother was German, and yet she was one of the cleverest girls at our school.

That autumn was particularly gloomy. In fact, the first year of the war was most depressing. It became known as 'the phoney war', but in a strange way it was every bit as nerve-racking as what was to follow. We all felt that our endurance would be strained to the limit before peace came again, but we didn't know what to expect, and it was not knowing that was frightening. And then, everyone was going away. At every station there were couples locked in each other's arms in a last farewell. In the blackout it looked even more devastating.

I felt particularly sorry for mothers of young children. Not everyone could bear to send them away to safety in the country, but it was devastating to see the small sad faces peering from the trains in the London railway stations, and the image of toddlers going away with their gas masks will be forever in our memories.

Tom went away after his eighteenth birthday in the spring and I didn't want to stay on at college any longer. With my friends, Lyn and Cynthia, I moved to Oakley Street, near the Thames in Chelsea. We had no problem getting jobs and, by the late spring of 1940, we were women of the world with our own apartments, if that's not too grand a description of bedsitting rooms with gas rings.

At the time, being Irish, I was in the war, but not of it. I was prepared to face anything that happened, but it was not my war, although there was the dreaded possibility of Ireland losing her independence again should the Nazis win the war.

Compared with my friends, I had one reason for feeling grateful. My family was safe in Ireland, and I was sorry for the people whose families were in constant danger.

Dunkirk

liners, barges, cruisers, yawls

frigates, destroyers, sloops and trawlers

ships of every shape and size

are sailing to France.

The men on the beach straffed and

                      machine-gunned

desperately await the armada

of yachtsmen, fishermen, navalmen,

sailors of every description under heaven

who are running gunnels under

              to Dunkirk.

A Nightingale Sang

Chapter 3

1940

On the continent the Allies were doing badly. The Maginot Line, France's main line of defence against Germany, reached only as far as the Belgian border, and now the German army had marched beyond its limits and would soon reach the Channel coast.

These were traumatic days for Britain and at the end of May, Lord Gort was instructed to bring the British Expeditionary Force home. There was every reason to believe that it would be needed to defend the island against an invading army.

Dunkirk, to the east of Calais, was chosen as the port of evacuation for the British Expeditionary Force and the remnants of the French and Belgian armies. Nine terrible days followed, when the men were under constant attack from the enemy army and air force.

"Where's the bloody R.A.F. we kept shouting," one of our friends told us when he arrived, dirty and dishevelled, at the home of my school friend Hazel, where I was spending the weekend. In his confused mind, he had left the train at Haywards Heath and walked to London. He thought of his friends and he wanted to see them.

Later I heard of the big wild Westport man, Regimental Sergeant Major Joe Mulroy. He led his men out to a waiting barge, holding his rifle at full stretch above his head. With the water up to his chest, he encouraged them, bellowing profanities as only he could, and he got them all aboard. He was awarded the British Empire Medal for bravery.

Every man coming home had his own story to tell. They trudged down to the promenade, weary beyond words after days of marching; behind them the inferno that was Dunkirk and, in front, a black sea fraught with danger. Out there, so far away, but as near as it was realistically possible for them to approach, were craft of every description under heaven.

Winston Churchill was Prime Minister now and when he called for volunteer boat owners to join the naval armada which would lift the men from the Dunkirk beaches, they came in their hundreds – nearly seven hundred privately-owned boats, we heard. Between them they brought back to England well over three hundred thousand men; all they could lift of the forces of Britain, France and Belgium who had gone out to meet the pride of Hitler's Wehrmacht over the previous nine months.

Operation Dynamo was the code name chosen for the evacuation of the British Expeditionary Force, and the order for its commencement went out on the evening of the 24th May. It lasted until the 2nd June and succeeded, against all the odds because of a vigorous rear-guard action by British troops before Dunkirk. Also, in spite of the 'Royal Absent

Friends' description of the R.A.F. by the anxious troops on the beaches, one hundred and seventy-six German planes were shot down during the evacuation.

At midnight on the 2nd June, the last three thousand British and French troops sailed away from the French coast. Four long turbulent years would pass before they could return.

A Nightingale Sang

It's a deadly cacophony

A murderous symphony

An unending display of man's inhumanity

This battle for London

A Nightingale Sang

Chapter 4

1940

London's 'phoney war' ended with a bang halfway through August, when about fifteen hundred enemy planes flew in over the Straits of Dover headed for the capital. It was the start of the Battle of Britain – a battle for air supremacy; a softening up before Hitler's proposed invasion.

Every available aircraft was involved in the battle, with Biggin Hill aerodrome playing a major role. Exhausted airmen took to the skies, fighting for their own homes and their own families, but ably assisted by the Polish airmen who were refugees from Hitler's aggression in their homeland. They were known to bail out a doomed aircraft and immediately take off in another. There was a shortage of men and planes, but those who were there fought with incredible courage and tenacity over the coming months. They became 'the Few' of Winston Churchill's famous speech, to whom so many owed so much.

They were the 'Brylcreem Boys', the glamour boys of the forces who took their lives in their hands every day. They commended their comrades with shouts of 'Good show!' and 'Wizard Prang!' and sympathized in their own way when 'old so-and-so bought it'. They were flamboyant and they were brave. Their expectation of life during those awful months was said to be about seven days.

Among the thousands of airmen who lost their lives at that time were two of the grammar school boys who had helped to make the church services more interesting for the convent girls when I was at school. They would zoom up to the church door on their motorbikes, making as much noise as they could. They'd swagger into church, unrolling the long scarves which were popular with their kind. They were so full of life and energy, how could we have guessed that their lives would end so tragically, and so soon?

Among the fallen was my dear quiet friend, Willy Palmer from over the hill at home, who joined the Royal Air Force. I remember him standing unnoticed at our back door, smiling at our noisy family. He was already talking about getting married.

"But we've hardly lived yet," I said. "There'll be plenty of time when the fighting is over. We'll have our whole lives ahead."

A year later he was dead, one of the crew of an outdated Fairey Battle light bomber shot down on a suicide mission to blow up the bridge at Maastricht to prevent the advance of the Germans into Holland in 1940. All but one of the planes was destroyed. I dreamt of him that night. I saw the plane spiralling down out of a black sky. Willy Brabazon-Palmer, dead before he was twenty years old.

More than twelve hundred civilians had been killed before the Battle of London started on the 8th September

Chapter 4 - 1940

1940. The blitzkrieg was Hitler's next move and it was meant to have such a devastating effect on Londoners that they would call for an end to the war.

The East End, with the docks area, took the brunt of the bombing to start with. Night and day they came over. There was no respite, no rest for anyone. Everyday became a challenge – us against them. But we were young. Life was sweet and we had to survive. There was something to be thankful for every morning.

The ferocious dogfights continued through most of September, but in the end German losses in the daylight were too heavy to sustain, and from October onwards the raiders came only at night.

I had reason to remember the night of the 15th September, when I was returning from a visit to a friend in Croydon. The warning sounded and the train stopped before Victoria for what seemed ages. The night sky was alight with flashes of gunfire and the fires started by incendiary bombs. It was a massive fireworks display, and a murderous one.

There was chaos when we finally arrived at Victoria Station, where a German plane had crashed in the forecourt. The underground was crowded with people sheltering and I decided to walk to Sloane Square, my next station.

I was anxious to get home, but it was a hair-raising walk. Every few minutes a shower of flak would clatter onto the street, and I would press myself into a doorway and wait until the screech of a descending bomb ended in a might explosion. With thuds and explosions and the constant crackle of gunfire, I felt that my eardrums would burst.

I tried to detach myself from the incredible noise and confusion by imagining that I was a footpad prowling alone through the dimly-lit alleyways of Victorian London, but time and again the familiar whine of a descending bomb sent me scurrying for the shelter of a doorway.

The blackout that I hated was relieved to some extent by a bombers' moon. Did that mean that when the bomb-aimers looked down to decide where to drop their deadly load, they could see me scurrying through the rows of Belgravia's elegant houses, I wondered? In my solitary game, I became the target for the Luftwaffe that night and, when an air raid warden called out to me in Sloane Square, I scuttled like a frightened rabbit for the shelter of the underground station.

When I eventually arrived at the house, Cynthia and her young sister were crouching under a table in the basement. They were relieved to see me and, somewhat unreasonably, I felt safe now that I was home. We celebrated with a cup of tea, as usual.

Outside, the unholy hell of exploding bombs and gunfire continued unabated until the early hours of the morning. It was said that over a thousand bombers and fighters came over that night and, by the end of the month, thousands of civilians had been killed in London. However, now some of the theatres were reopening. It was important to keep up the morale of the people. One theatre had its dressing rooms bombed the night it opened and the cast changed on the stage. Londoners enjoyed showing that they could 'take it'. The Windmill Theatre, with its comedians and strip shows, boasted that it 'NEVER CLOSED'.

The air raids dominated our lives. Death and destruction continued and we began to take it in our stride. In Oakley Street, Chelsea, where we lived, we had dragged our mattresses down to the basement and we pulled a large cupboard in front of the window to prevent being hit by flying glass.

During the winter German bombers targeted industrial areas. Coventry was destroyed. It gave a new word to the Germans. 'Koventrieran' became the description of razing to the ground. In Liverpool, Britain's gateway to the Atlantic, the surviving ships of a convoy sailed into the harbour which was being hammered with its two-hundredth air raid. In one week, after four consecutive nights of bombing, thirteen merchant ships were destroyed.

At the same time, the air raids continued night after night in London, up to the end of January. We had almost become accustomed to the sleepless nights and sleep-walking days when they stopped, just as suddenly as they had begun.

We couldn't believe it at first. The quiet nights were disturbing. We were waiting for the sirens and could hardly sleep for the silence. But life began to come back to normal. We would dance again; we would love and laugh like before.

Evidently Hitler had decided that Britain's merchant ships were her lifeline and attacks on them intensified. The

U-boats were now the biggest menace. The drastic naval losses continued to be a nightmare and Winston Churchill was in deadly earnest when he told the Commons, "Day after day, we are fighting for our lives."

Britain couldn't survive without the vital supplies from across the Atlantic, and the twin pocket battleships *Scharnhorst* and *Gneisenau* were the bane of the seamen sailing the North Atlantic. Every day we read of terrible losses at sea, but at home the quiet nights continued and our social lives resumed where they had left off.

Nineteen-forty rang the knell

for neighbours, friends and relatives,

the boy beside me in the school

who smiled at my fear of eternity.

Scared of a time without an end

scared of a place without a friend

you were nonplussed that I should see

beyond a weekend free from school.

But yesterday

two years from school

a U-boat man took careful aim

and whisked you to eternity.

A Nightingale Sang

Chapter 5

1941

The river and the Kings Road made Chelsea a great place to live, but rents were higher than in the outer suburbs. Across the street from Norway House and the Northern Ireland Office pay was higher in Canada House, so I was delighted to get a job there and often joined the others for a drink in Scotts in Piccadilly. It was there I met Roger Sands who, from the start, made no secret of the fact that he was attracted to 'the little Irish girl'. The following day there was a note on my desk inviting me to have dinner with him.

Known as Sandy, he was a psychiatrist with the rank of captain in the Canadian Army. He had qualified in New York and had gone back to Toronto just a year before the war. He was ten years older than I was, but I believed this was going to be a platonic friendship during what could turn out to be a long war.

One morning, I was delighted to get a telephone call from Sandy.

"Where've you been? I haven't seen you for ages," he said.

"Dodging bombs like everyone else, I suppose."

"Well, I think we've spent enough nights looking at the four walls. I want to see you," he said. "I'll come over your way. I'll call you and we can have a drink at the Six Bells."

"That'll be great. I'll look forward to seeing you," I said.

It was the 7th March 1941 and we hadn't had a raid since the beginning of February. Maybe London's dark nightmare was over.

I was standing on the doorstep breathing in the good fresh air. There was a soft breeze blowing off the river and I had the feeling that spring was just around the corner. I hurried down the steps and hopped over the large water pipe that ran down to the Thames as a wartime measure against the fires.

As soon as I arrived at the office, the telephone rang. It was Sandy.

"And how are you this fine morning?"

There were minor eruptions in the pit of my stomach at the sound of his voice.

"Many happy returns of the day," he said.

"How did you know?"

"Oh, I have ways of finding out. I'd like to cook a meal for you tonight if you'll come to the apartment." So far we had steered clear of his apartment. "I'd love to," I said, "and thank you."

"I've had a food parcel from Canada and I'd like you to share it. I'm having a working lunch, but I'll see you in the lobby after 5.30."

I was glad Greg had said we had a busy day ahead. Anything to make the day go faster.

Sandy had a studio apartment in a big Victorian house in Holland Park. There was a large comfortably furnished bed-sitting room with a small kitchen and bathroom. It was warm, but he put a light to the gas poker which was a permanent fixture under the logs in the grate. Soon they were blazing. He opened a bottle of champagne and we had two glasses before he went into the kitchen. Obviously everything had been prepared in advance. I was impressed.

It was a lovely meal. "This is heavenly," I said. "I didn't know that cooking was among your many talents."

"I got the best cookbook London had to offer and followed it to the letter. I'm glad you appreciate my efforts."

"It's superb," I said and kissed him.

Our rationed food was basic now. We had the bare essentials to keep us healthy. Tenpence worth of meat for a week. That would be, maybe, two small lamb cutlets or a little beef for stewing. We had two ounces of butter and some margarine. I couldn't get used to the margarine. When the butter was finished, I would spread the marge and fry or toast the bread. It didn't seem quite as bad like that.

We were entitled to one egg every month, but it wasn't always available, and we had half a pint of milk delivered every other day. There was plenty of rather grey bread and a couple of ounces of cheese, and very little else. We could buy apples sometimes, but you would have to be pregnant to get orange juice, and bananas were available only to children with a certain deficiency.

I had every reason to enjoy the meal Sandy had just cooked and when it was over I sat on the rug and sang an Irish song that he liked:

> *'Like sunrise on the Wicklow Hills*
> *You set my heart aglow....'*

"I like a girl who sings for her supper," he said. "But I made myself a promise this morning. I said that if you agreed to come over here tonight..." (He actually said, "If you did me the honour ....") "...I wouldn't ask you to stay."

"I won't deny that I want to stay," I said, but I'm not going to." Sandy was married – something that had been mentioned only once, and I wanted to avoid getting badly hurt in the future. I didn't want to hurt his feelings either, so I kissed him again. "Of course I want to stay," I said. "But I'm trying to be sensible."

"I know," he said. "And you're probably right. I'll take you home. Tomorrow night we'll dance at the Café de Paris. O.K? I know you like it. I'll meet you at Scotts at six. We'll have a drink first."

"Did you know that the Café de Paris was once a bear pit?" I asked Sandy.

"No one ever tells me anything," he said.

Chapter 5 - 1941

"Well, I'll tell you something else. The ballroom was remodelled as an exact replica of the ballroom on the *Titanic*. I hope it will have a happier ending."

"You're a mine of information" he said. "What would I do without you? I don't think you should go home tonight."

"Neither do I, but don't make it any more difficult."

I couldn't sleep. Why hadn't I stayed with Sandy. Would he ask me again? Would I go on refusing? Could I? Supposing the war lasts for years, what would happen to us then? Oh, I'd have to think about that tomorrow. Then I remembered that I'd refused because I didn't want to be hurt and I went to sleep feeling virtuous.

Sandy was my first thought in the morning. Tonight I would meet him for a drink in Scotts and then we'd go to the Café de Paris for dinner and dancing. I loved that place. Ken Johnson, a handsome Caribbean who was generally known as *Snakehips*, had one of the best dance bands in Town and there was always a great atmosphere. Being underground and sound-proofed, we could forget about the bombs, if there were any. Then I would definitely go home. There'd be no staying out tonight.

It was after eight when we arrived at the Café de Paris and the band played while we had dinner, but everyone was waiting for Snakehips, and there was loud applause when he arrived.

"It's hell out there," he said to someone as he walked up to the stage. "They've started again."

A murmur went all the way round the dining room. Everyone was shocked and disappointed. We had come to enjoy the quiet nights and now we would have to face the noise and danger all over again. But for now we were underground and safe, weren't we?

Snakehips hopped on to the stage and we got up to dance. The tempo of the music increased and dancers filled the small floor. Sandy was an excellent dancer and I enjoyed jiving to 'Cherry Pink Mambo'. I wanted to be happy. Everyone wanted to be happy – to enjoy the night, so we had to believe we were in the safest place in London.

"Play 'Oh Johnnie'," Snakehips called to the band, and the dancers sang the familiar words – "how you can love" as others crowded on to the floor. The place was alive with the hilarity that was typical of young people in wartime London. Somebody said that everyone in London was in love during the war and there was certainly no shortage of lovers.

"It's hot in here," Sandy said. "Come up on the balcony."

I hated to leave the floor, but I followed reluctantly as he edged his way to our table to retrieve my jacket. Before we got there, all hell broke loose. I couldn't remember hearing an explosion. There was a lot of noise anyway and I was thrown back on something soft. Sandy picked me up.
"Are you alright?" he said.
"Yes, I'm o.k." I was shaking.

Chapter 5 - 1941

There was still a light shining on the balcony, but everywhere else was in complete darkness. There was an enormous cloud of dust and an evil smell. The volume of noise had increased with ear-splitting cries of agony and people shouting out names in the dark, trying to find their friends, with the urgency of fear and anxiety.

"Come on," Sandy said, catching my hand and groping in the dark for the exit. As we left, the staff were already going around with torches trying to assess the situation. A few people were holding up cigarette lighters.

"No naked lights, please, there may be gas," someone yelled.

Already we knew that most of the damage was on the dance floor and possibly on the stage. Upstairs there was confusion. The streets were blocked and people were crowding round the entrance, which was open and showing some light, in spite of the blackout. Maybe the doors had been blown away.

"The ambulance can't get through," someone said, and members of the staff were commandeering the taxis as they came along, for the walking wounded.

"We'll never get a cab tonight," Sandy said. "I'll try to get a room at the Regent Palace," and he looked at me enquiringly. "Come on, we'll have a drink there. We need one."

We stumbled over heaps of rubble and took the short walk slowly, dodging into doorways once or twice. To Sandy's relief, we managed to get a room. I no longer felt capable of making a decision.

"If you'd like to leave your clothes out, we'll look after them," the receptionist said, and for the first time we saw that we were covered in dust and plaster. We had baths while we waited and I washed and towel-dried my hair which was thick with dust. An hour later, we were down in the bar. It was crowded. Dozens of people were coming in from the Café de Paris and everyone was anxious to see that they got seats. The waiters were leaving bottles of wine and glasses on the tables.

We were told that Ken Johnson and some of the band had been killed, as well as dozens of dancers. Some people said hundreds, but nobody seemed to know for certain. There had been a second bomb which, fortunately, had not exploded, but had burst on the floor, spewing a filthy yellow substance around.

I saw someone I knew coming in with a party. This was the pretty Welsh girl, Helen, I used to meet at the Overseas Club. Her grandmother had given her a leopard skin coat for her twenty-first birthday recently and I was surprised to see that she wasn't wearing it, knowing it to be her pride and joy. I went across to speak to her.

She was covered in dust and had obviously come from the Café. "I didn't see you there," I said.

"We've just left. Megan here is a nurse so she's been busy," she said by way of introduction. "The Canadian nurses are doing Trojan work over there."

Megan looked exhausted. The thick coating of dust and plaster in her hair gave her a ghostly look.

"How long have you been in London?" I asked her.

"I arrived two days ago," she said. "We were told that the worst of the blitz was over, but they must have known we were coming. There were several hundred nurses on board and I'd say most of them have been busy tonight."

I've no doubt people are grateful to you all," I said. "Let's hope you won't have too many nights like this."

"I had to put my coat around a girl whose clothes had been blown off. She was about to go into the street," Helen said.

"Will you get it back?" I asked, anxious for her.

"Oh, I will. I put an envelope with my address and telephone number in the pocket. I made sure she understood that. Someone wrapped a tablecloth around another girl. The ambulances were very slow coming. I suppose the streets are blocked, but people were angry. Most of the injured had to be taken to the hospitals in taxis.

"We'll miss our lovely bandleader, won't we Fran?"

"Oh, I can't believe it." I thought of the urbane and exotic Snakehips, like a bronze young god, shattered in the blast.

"Dave Williams was killed as well. Did you know?"

"We heard a few members of the band had been killed, but no one knew exactly who they were, apart from

Snakehips. It's too awful," I said, although the truth had hardly hit home yet.

It should have been comforting to be with Sandy, but I lay in his arms stunned by the sudden deaths of the dancers and music-makers; of laughter turned to agonising screams. I felt that we would never laugh again. Our thoughts were on the terrible destruction down the street – so many killed who had gone out to enjoy an evening's dancing. It was impossible to think of making love. I lay awake for hours while the raid continued. Poor old London, and we thought the bombing had stopped.

I had just fallen into an uneasy sleep when I was startled by the loud clanging of the telephone.

"Seven-thirty, your morning call, sir". I didn't know Sandy had asked for a call, but, as though we had just become aware of each other, we made love and some of the tensions of the night eased away.

I heard him call my name, but the diminutive 'Francie' that he had used the night before for the first time. No one ever called me that. I thought he said "I love you." Out loud he said, "God knows how we're here and in one piece. We should have been on that dance floor."

We walked the short distance to work. I held his hand, anxious for the physical contact we had enjoyed. He looked slightly withdrawn, his mind already on the business of the day. I was disappointed. It had been ecstatic, I thought. How did Sandy feel about making love, I wondered? He was so much older and more experienced. Was it like a soft summer shower compared with the excitement of the storm at sea which I had experienced?

I wished we could talk about it, but when we got to Trafalgar Square, he kissed me on the cheek. Then, sensing my disappointment, he hugged me and kissed me again. "Halfpint," he said, smiling at my serious face. It was his name for me when he wanted to tease. "I'll call you during the day."

"Don't go yet, please. Can we sit on the seat here just for a few minutes. I'm not ready to face the day yet."

We sat down. "Why don't you take the day off? You're entitled to it after what's happened. I'll ring Greg."

"No, no. I don't want to be alone. I'll have a cup of coffee here and then I'll be fine. I'd rather be busy. Thank you for everything. It was wonderful."

"No, thank you honey. Do you know what a difference you make to my life in London?" He kissed me again.

I felt happy then in spite of the disastrous consequences of the bombing.

A Nightingale Sang

Chapter 6

1941

News of Ken Johnson's death at twenty-six shocked London, especially the young dancers, but the lengthening days helped me to recover my good spirits. Although Coventry Street and Piccadilly were cleared of rubble in record time after the bombing, it was rumoured that the Café de Paris would never re-open and the ugly hoarding around the site added to the growing number of London's scars.

The air raids continued and night-life tended to be confined to weekends and special occasions, but everyone seemed to be more cheerful. There was a hint of triumphalism in the air; a feeling that they had not done so badly since the fall of France. Even after Dunkirk, which some people might have called a retreat, the British felt only pride in having rescued three hundred and fifty thousand men from the jaws of death or imprisonment. That was the spirit that convinced us all of their ultimate victory. Didn't Winston Churchill tell them, "If the British Empire were to last a thousand years, men would still say 'This was their finest hour'"?

At home we owed a debt of gratitude to a trio of unexpected bomb disposal experts known as the Holy Trinity. They were the Earl of Suffolk and his secretary –a very brave lady – and his chauffeur. They did some splendid work over several months until their luck ran out and they were blown to bits by a bomb they were diffusing in Erith in Kent.

In spite of the bombs, we celebrated St. Patrick's Day in Oakley Street. We managed to accumulate a rare selection of liquor, including a bottle of 'Irish whisky' which one of my friends had brought from Freetown in Sierra Leone. A Union Jack dominated the label, which shows how little the world knew about us. The taste was indescribable. No wonder Irish whiskey had a bad name in England. I felt I should start a campaign in support of the genuine home product.

Anyway the mixture of alcoholic drinks was lethal, and with only Ry-Vita and cheese as blotting paper, everyone got very merry and our medley of Irish airs competing with bombs and guns produced an interesting cacophony over the Thames that night. We had intended to go dancing, but it was a hostile world outside so we settled for the comfort of my room.

The raids continued through April and the river, so often a moonlit trail for the bombers, brought Chelsea more than its share of destruction. Halfway through the month we had a seriously heavy raid when the Old Church was bombed and older residents were leaving the borough in tens of thousands, while we, being young, were convinced of our indestructibility.

We read that seven hundred bombers came over on the night of the 16th April, killing a thousand people and injuring twice as many.

Altogether, there was very little good news coming in. The British had evacuated Benghazi, and Rommel was continuing to advance in North Africa. Greece had surrendered and the fall of Crete was imminent.

The sad news from home was that two of four brothers who had served on the *Gloucester* had gone down with their ship off Crete. Naturally the news had upset the entire neighbourhood.

The news from the Mediterranean was altogether disastrous. Three cruisers and eight destroyers had been sunk; two battleships, *Warspite* and *Barham* were seriously damaged and the aircraft carrier *Formidable* had to be withdrawn from service. In addition, five cruisers and seven destroyers were severely damaged. More than two thousand officers and men of the Royal Navy were killed or lost at sea and just under five hundred were wounded. And all the damage had been inflicted by aircraft. The Italian fleet never left port.

Naturally Admiral Cunningham, the Commander-in-Chief, declared that he had never experienced so much tension and anxiety. In addition to the Cretan problem, he was concerned about besieged Malta as well as supplies to the desert army and Tobruk.

The whole Eastern Mediterranean was open to an Axis attack when fate intervened and induced Hitler to attack Russia. Why did he choose that time? Cecil Rhodes, in his time, would not have been the only one to believe God wanted as much of the world as possible painted British-red.

The good news was that May came in bright and sunny, and the longer days would mean less time for the night raiders, and now that Hitler was obviously diverting some of his attention to Russia, there was a hope that the blitz would not last forever.

On these pleasant evenings my colleague, Diana, and I would walk the length of Piccadilly on our way home from work, singing 'Praise the Lord and pass the ammunition' and anything else that came into our minds, while Londoners passed by without a sideways glance. Yes, most of the time we were happy enough.

The first Saturday morning in May Sandy rang early.
"It's a lovely day, why don't we go out of town?"
"I'd love that. We could go now and have a nice long day. There's some pleasant country around Aylesbury."
"Fine. Are you ready? I'll meet you at South Kensington."

We took the train to Aylesbury and had lunch. Then, after a long walk, we reached the quiet fields beyond the town. It was so peaceful, it helped to forget our nightly bombardment. London was another world.

"Lyn and I picked mushrooms out here last August," I said. "We ate them with our bacon ration when we got home. It was a feast fit for a king. I was reminded of it when I saw that couple picking something from the hedgerows over there. It's too early for blackberries. I wonder what they're picking. It might be May blossom. It's lovely in a vase, but in Ireland they say it's unlucky to bring it into the house. I wonder why?" But I was talking to myself. My companion was too sleepy to answer and I too gave in to temptation and decided to lie in the sun and let the world go by. It was a quiet day, a balm for the soul; a day to remember when the bombs would be a thing of the past.

"We must do this more often," Sandy said.
"You mean sleep?"
"Love is all the more desirable for having slept and sleep is all the easier for having loved. There is time for both here, isn't there?" Yes, it was a day to remember.

With the warmer weather coming, I could look forward to wearing some pretty clothes again. We were almost in uniform now with so few clothing coupons, but I had bought three summer dresses in the new 'Guinea Shops' which had opened just before the war and these were still my stand-by for the warmer days. I could get away from the strict orders which applied to the new clothes; knee-length skirts with no more than three pleats, jackets with no more than three buttons and heels no higher than one and a half inches.

I liked high heels and I was delighted when Sandy found some lovely shoes in a theatrical shop where they didn't ask for coupons. I made a mental note that it was in Shaftesbury Avenue. I would remember that the next time I wanted shoes for dancing.

Many of us got our legs tanned, either naturally or artificially as soon as we could, to save coupons on stockings, and we were always glad to acquire defunct parachutes which could be made into pretty silk camiknickers with the addition of some lace. Most people managed to have a lively social life, so we found ingenious ways of keeping up a bit of style. Evening wear was seen only on the most formal occasions.

Mothers and grannies were persuaded to raid their sewing boxes for fancy buttons that could be painted with nail varnish and glued on to clips which were available in the shops, to be used as ear-rings. Ladders in silk stockings could be mended professionally, although some girls had the patience to do their own with a tiny crochet-hook type of thing.

We all knitted dresses as well as sweaters, sometimes with 2-ply wool and thin needles. This was hard work, but it was all part of the struggle to look good.

Now that Greece had surrendered, I was anxiously wondering what had happened to the marines who had been stationed there, thinking of my friend Tom Faulkener from Holborn. It seemed such a long time ago. Tom had been gone two years and I hadn't heard from him for several months, but I guessed that his last letter had come from Greece. Then we knew that when Greece fell, thousands of men had been evacuated to Crete. Maybe Tom was among them. After that, it was only a matter of days before Crete was invaded by German paratroops and another massive evacuation was forced upon the Allies.

On the spur of the moment I decided to ring Tom's parents, although I had not met them. His mother answered the telephone.

"My name is Frances Carolan, Mrs. Faulkener. I was at college with Tom. We were writing to each other, but I haven't heard from him for a long time now. I was wondering if you have any news."

"How nice to hear from you Frances. I remember your name. We love to hear from any of Tom's friends, but we haven't heard from him for some time either. We believe he was on Crete, so naturally, we're worried. Maybe you'd let me have your telephone number and I'll ring you if we hear anything."
"Are you still at college?"
"No, I didn't want to stay on after they'd all gone away. I'm living in Chelsea now – Oakley Street. The telephone number is FLAxman 2893."
"If you're ever in this area Frances, we'd be delighted to see you. We miss the boys so much. My eldest son is in North Africa. That's another worry."
"Yes it is. Thank you for your invitation. Tom was a particular friend of mine."
Oh, I remember now. You're the Irish girl he was so fond of. He'd be delighted if you could manage to spend a weekend with us. Do try."

"I will indeed. Thank you again."

It would be nice to spend a weekend in the Shirley Hills, and safer than Chelsea, I imagine. We'd had a particularly bad raid the night before, killing about fifteen hundred people and damaging the Houses of Parliament.

In the morning, before I left for work, I had a telephone call from Helen, the Welsh girl who'd been at the Café de Paris when it was bombed.

"Did you get your coat back?" was my first question.
"Oh yes, with a box of chocolates that must have cost the whole family's sweet coupons for a month. I've been wondering if we could meet one evening. Friday would suit me."
"Friday's fine," I would be spending the weekend with Sandy, so I would be free on Friday night.
"I could meet you outside Swan & Edgars after work and we could eat in Soho maybe?"
"Lovely. See you then," I said.
We went to Leongs and Helen was full of her plans to join the WAAF, the Women's' Air Force.

"I volunteered shortly after the café bombing and I'm going at the end of next week. That's why I wanted to see you. I'm hoping to meet all my friends before I go away. Where are you dancing these days, by the way?"

"We go to Quaglino's mostly, or the Hungaria, but it's not the same. I suppose we'll get over Snakehips in time.

There was such a great atmosphere in that place. It looks awful now with the hoarding in front, and they say it will never re-open."

"Oh, I still have nightmares about that night. I think you missed the worst sights. I had to stay on with Megan, but you did have an attentive companion. He's been around for some time now, hasn't he? Are we going to have a wedding?"

"No, it's just a wartime romance, I'm afraid."

"Well I'm sorry to hear that. I thought you looked good together."

"Yes, we have a lot of fun. We're both trying to keep it like that. There's no future in it, I'm sorry to say."

Helen looked at me expectantly, but I didn't encourage her to ask any more questions. "Oh, there's Moaning Minny half an hour early," she said when the sirens sounded. "We'd better be going home. I hope it's not as bad as last night. Good luck and keep out of harm's way."

"You too," I said.

The gunfire had already started when we left the restaurant and we hurried to the tube station, where we parted company and I rode the few stations to South Kensington alone.

It was noisy now, and I felt more apprehensive than usual about the mile-long walk to Oakley Street. In the dark I hurried through Onslow Square. There was no one about. I had just reached Fulham Road and was watching the searchlights scanning the dark sky, showing up the black silhouettes of the bombers and occasional bursts of gunfire, when there was an ominous whistle. I crouched down on the pavement, covering my head as well as I could with my arms. The bomb dropped, followed by the clatter of bricks and breaking glass. I felt an excruciating pain in my back and passed out momentarily. I came to with a lot of people talking. Something hurt like hell.

"We want to make you comfortable, love. The ambulance is coming." A policeman was bending over me.

"Why, where am I?" I thought I'd been asleep in bed.

"You'll be alright love." He put his arms around me and I wished he wouldn't. It felt heavy.

The ambulance took me to Charing Cross Hospital, which was busy. They dressed the wound, gave me painkillers and put me to bed.

In the morning Lyn left nightclothes and my toilet bag. They were strict about visiting hours, but the girls came over the following few evenings and Sandy brought books to cheer me up; Damon Runyon and Thorne Smith.

The wound healed quickly on the surface and I expected to go home, but the doctor thought otherwise.

"The left kidney is inflamed. You had a heavy blow. We're sending you out to Ashridge in Hertfordshire. There'll be an ambulance leaving tomorrow."

Chapter 6 - 1941

There was no point in protesting so I buried my head in the pillow and cried instead. It was bad enough being in hospital, I thought, but being buried alive in the wilds of Hertfordshire was something else. I didn't want to leave London. Ashridge was a college in peacetime, the nurses told me. It was converted to hospital use for the severely wounded from Dunkirk and for evacuees from the London hospitals.

In the morning, several patients on stretchers were laid side by side in the courtyard to wait for the ambulance, which was a converted Green Line bus. The man lying next to me smiled kindly, but I turned my head away. I couldn't force a smile.

When the bus arrived, I, being the lightest, was the first to be strapped up under the roof. Halfway to Ashridge the driver stopped, went into a café and brought out tea for everyone. He refused any payment.

"I have my own reasons for doing it," he said, and everyone loved him. We were all anxious to know the reason for his generosity, but he wasn't telling. Had someone brought him tea when he needed it badly, I wondered, or his wife, or his mother? We would all like to have heard the story and we told him we would never forget him.

I was put into a ward with other young people. The little girl opposite sang 'You are my sunshine' all day long. I had never liked the song, but now it became an abomination.

While I was in hospital, we heard that the *Gloucester* had sunk during the evacuation. A letter from home, which Lyn had sent on, confirmed that two of our near neighbours had gone down with the ship. There were four brothers serving in the Royal Navy and now two of them were lost. What terrible news for their parents, and indeed for the village.

I would come to think of that period in hospital as the quietest time of my life. I slept a lot, but even when I was awake I didn't want to talk. I have loved singing all my life. I can't remember a time when I could resist giving a song, but on the day they decided to have a concert in the ward, I didn't even sit up. I didn't want to be part of anything.

I couldn't deny that my back was painful, but neither could I believe that the condition was all that serious, but they kept me there for six weeks – in bed. I could hardly walk when I got up. The muscles in the back of my legs didn't seem to work and I thought I was falling over backwards. That's how I felt the day one of the doctors drove me to Berkhamsted, to the nearest railway station. He put me on a train for Euston.

"No wild parties now," he said as I was leaving. I'll have to learn to walk before I can dance again, I thought.

My next letter from home had the sad news that a boy from my first school, who was a radio officer on a merchant ship, was reported lost. I remembered telling him when we were seven or eight that I was afraid of eternity. I didn't like the teacher telling us that something was going to last forever, especially if it wasn't good. He said it didn't scare him. Now I hoped it would be happy for him. He hadn't had long to enjoy this world.

As well as the *Gloucester*, the papers reported the loss of the cruiser *Fiji* and four destroyers off Crete. Lord Mountbatten's ship, *HMS Kelly*, was among them, but apparently he was able to swim free. These losses and the subsequent loss of the 'unsinkable' battleship *Hood,* with all but three of her huge complement of men, compelled the Prime Minister to issue the dramatic order to '*Sink the Bismarck'*. This was taken up by several ships, including the aircraft carrier *Ark Royal* and the battleships *King George V* and *Rodney*. With several smaller ships, they formed a ring around the *Bismarck* in mid-Atlantic, battering her on all quarters until the larger ships sailed for home, leaving the cruiser *Dorsetshire* to finish her off with three torpedoes.

It was the 27th May, 1941, and we hadn't had a raid since the 11th. Once again we hoped that the blitz was over.

I was no sooner out of hospital than I had a telephone call from home telling me that my cousin had been killed on the airfield on which he was stationed in Yorkshire. That meant going up there straight away. Several men had been killed, including the Commanding Officer, but George's funeral was delayed to allow time for his mother to arrive from Ireland. It was a sad journey for her. She had lost her husband in the First World War. I thought of the quote from the bible, 'He was the only son of his mother and she was a widow.'

Guns were fired and the Last Post was sounded at George's funeral. I found it extremely emotional and wondered how my aunt could survive such a dramatic ceremony. I was sad to think of him being buried under this Yorkshire hillside, so far from home, when I heard that his father was born not many miles from here. I was surprised that my aunt hadn't mentioned it, but I didn't want to remind her of another sad event. George would have had only hazy memories of his father.

Greg Horan, my boss, had suggested that I should take a couple of extra days off to travel back to Ireland with my aunt. It was lovely to see everyone at home, although they were upset to have lost so many of the local boys. Apart from the devastated parents, our local postmistress was very distressed at having to deliver so many sad messages. She felt obliged to deliver the telegrams personally and she confided to someone that she would resign rather than face so much sadness again.

Those who saw their loved ones leave for the war tried to prepare themselves for the worst that life could offer, but fortunately for us, hope is always stronger than fear. Nevertheless we all slept with a prayer in our hearts.

This was a depressing time. There was a strange feeling of anti-climax after the blitz which was hard to put into words. No one was going to admit that they missed the excitement of fear, but, buoyed up as we were to face danger, it was hard to settle down to quiet nights again.

Chapter 6 - 1941

There had been a certain freedom about the last year, a time when the petty irritations were laid aside in a common bond to survive, but now our priorities had altered again and had more or less gone back to normal.

When I got back to London after the short Irish visit, Sandy was at Euston to meet me. It was a lovely surprise. At six o'clock in the morning I wasn't expecting to see anyone I knew there.

"You've had a rough time, haven't you?" He sounded so kind, I snuggled up closer to him in the back of the taxi. "I've been thinking that a weekend in Bournemouth would do you good. What do you think?"

"I love Bournemouth, but it's too close to my old school. I wouldn't like to run into any of the teachers, but a weekend by the sea would be lovely. What about Brighton? I really like it."

He laughed. Brighton had a reputation at that time.
"Sure, Brighton would be great. Less travelling and more time by the sea."

We stayed at a hotel on the seafront where we had a wonderful view of the Channel. It was the first time I'd been on the coast since the war started and there were big changes. It was impossible to forget what was happening across the water because the beaches were covered with rolls of barbed wire and along the promenade there were pillboxes with guns showing in the slits. Still, we enjoyed our early morning walks when the breeze blew in from the Channel, and the quiet evenings sitting with our drinks in the bay window of the bar.

It was in Brighton, more than anywhere else, that I enjoyed being with Sandy. I kept my thoughts to myself knowing there would be no alternative for us but to part in the end and that there would be no parting without grief; no loss without that deep well of loneliness. My comfort would have to be that the end was nowhere in sight. It belonged somewhere in the future, to a time we might never see.

The weekend in Brighton was a very special time for both of us, when we really got to know each other, and it ended all too soon.

Chapter 7

1941

Oakley Street, where we lived, runs between the Kings Road and where the Albert Bridge crosses the Thames in Chelsea, and sometimes on the fine evenings of early June 1941, we would walk along the Embankment to Chelsea bridge and return through Battersea Park. It was easy to forget about the war on those quiet evenings, but as the days passed, we noticed an increase in air activity.

Around about eight o'clock we would hear the distant thunder of hundreds, maybe thousands, of massive bombers and for several minutes the sky would be darkened. They were allied aircraft flying south to bomb the Ruhr and the Rhineland.

It was a reminder to us that the war, which should have been over one Christmas long ago, was now only gathering momentum. There was a poignancy about it too, a certainty that not all of them would return.

One Friday evening, I had just returned from one of these strolls, when Sandy rang.
"Are you taking advantage of the fine weather? You were out when I rang before."

"Oh, you should have been with us. It was heavenly in the park."

"Can you meet me in the morning, I want to show you something?"

"Of course," I said "Where?"

"I'll be at South Ken at ten-thirty," he said.

I walked to the station in the morning filled with curiosity about what I was going to see. Sandy was already there when I arrived.

"It's just along the street here," he said, and there it was, the loveliest house in a terrace of elegant white houses with black woodwork, shining brasses and bright colourful window boxes. I loved these London houses.

"What do you think of that?"

"It's gorgeous. Are you going to move?"

"Only if you'll come with me."

I was speechless. Moving in with him had never entered my head. Even in Brighton, I hadn't thought of it as a possibility. "I'd like a cup of coffee," I said.

"Don't you want to see the inside?"

"Of course I do, but I want to think first. It's tempting, but it's a big decision."

In the evening I talked to my friends. I had a problem trying to make up my mind and I didn't know whether I wanted encouragement or not.

"I couldn't refuse a house like that," Cynthia said, "not once I'd seen it," but Lyn, who was six years older, advised caution.

"Don't get hurt, honey," she said.

In the morning, I felt light-headed. I still hadn't made a decision, but the possibility of living with Sandy made the day seem brighter. I was walking on air. I would be crazy to refuse. Or would I? We had decided to have lunch at the zoo to spend a few hours strolling around the gardens because the weather was lovely and someone said the food was good.

"I shouldn't have sprung that proposition on you yesterday," Sandy said when we met. "I'm going to move into the house and your place will be there if and when you want it. I have no right to persuade you."

That was it. I didn't say I'd almost made up my mind to move. It seemed a much more sensible decision and I was grateful that he'd made it. I was planning to take my annual holiday in September and would wait until after that to decide my next move. I couldn't face any questioning at home. In fact, when I thought of my parents, the whole idea seemed preposterous. At the same time it never failed to amaze me that they could leave a young girl alone in London in wartime and expect her to remain innocent. Was it innocence on their part, or a complete faith in my good sense?

I was relieved now that I was not expected to make the big decision and we walked around hand-in-hand laughing at everything and nothing because it was a glorious day and we were happy. There were a lot of days like that and it was easy to forget that Sandy had a life in Canada. It belonged in the past and I found it too painful to think about.

In the early hours of the 22nd June, the first German bombs fell on Russian territory. The blitz had not had the effect of breaking London's spirit as Hitler had hoped, and now the proposed invasion of Britain had obviously been postponed. This change of plan, for whatever reason it had been made, we all saw as the salvation of the west.

Day after day now we read of the terrible atrocities in Russia, especially against the Jews. The numbers killed were horrifying, even judged by World War One standards, and when Churchill and Roosevelt met off Newfoundland in August, they decided that the Soviet Union should have all the help it needed.

Gradually posters began to appear in the underground stations demanding that Britain should 'OPEN THE SECOND FRONT NOW'. The British Communists were anxious about the fate of their Russian comrades. Throughout the summer, the Germans advanced towards Leningrad and the Red Army retreated. It was a continual reminder to us to be grateful that they were not tramping through England's towns and villages.

Late in the summer I was delighted to get a letter from Tom. He had not had my letter and didn't know that I had spoken to his mother. He had been on Crete when the German paratroops landed. He was one of a party of fifty or so which had become detached from the main regiment. It saved them from capture. They were picked up by an Allied ship and, naturally, they hoped they would be going back to the U.K. "Unfortunately," he said, "it was going to the Far East."

"I thought I'd be seeing you," he wrote. "A lot of the fellows did get home, but there's no hope for us at the moment. It was a big disappointment. I think about you all the time; dream of things that may never happen and wish I'd had the courage to tell you how I felt while there was still time. You're the only one I can write to."

I felt sad and sentimental because that was not the way I felt about Tom. I loved him as one of my best friends and I always thought he felt the same. Maybe he was lonely and wanted to feel that there was someone waiting at home. I thought they must all feel like that.

At the weekend Sandy asked me to go canoeing with him in Oxfordshire before the cold weather set in.

"Not if you're going to shoot the rapids like all those wild Canadians in the pictures," I said.
"Oh, come on, you'll love it."

Of course, I loved it, and I felt even better when it was over, to have tried something new and found it so exhilarating. We spent the evening walking around Oxford, soaking in the atmosphere and admiring the enthralling sights of that beautiful city. We were brimming over with energy and good spirits after our unusual day.

The news that American ships had been attacked at sea by the Germans now meant that a state of undeclared war existed between them, and we read that American warships had escorted a British convoy out of Halifax, Nova Scotia. In September, the first American-built 'Liberty ships' were delivered in Britain to replace the thousands of ships sunk in the Atlantic. It was a relief all round to have the support of that great power.

Still, ships delivering supplies to the Russian port of Murmansk were having a bad time, being constantly harassed by German ships and planes stationed in Norway. The battleship *Tirpitz* was holed up in Trondheim, her presence in Arctic waters a constant threat to the convoys going to Russia. Several attempts were made to put her out of action, most of them unsuccessful at that time.

At the end of November came the good news that the siege of Tobruk had been lifted at last, and that Rommel was in retreat. This was a great relief to the many families who'd had relatives out there for so long.

Coming up to Christmas 1941, Sandy decided to have a house-warming and I promised to be there to help him.

"Does that mean you're coming to live with me?" he asked, with that smile that always made me laugh.

"No, but I'll help with your house-warming party," I said.

"What more could I ask?" he responded.

We chose the following Saturday night for the party. It was the 6th of December 1941 These were lean times, but we managed to rustle up a fair amount of food and drink. Sandy produced the box of cheeses, Christmas cake and two bottles of Canadian rye which his grandmother had sent.

I thought the house looked particularly elegant on the night. It was attractively furnished in the Regency style except for a large modern white sofa in the sitting-room. It looked warm and welcoming with big fires, and that night we decided to use only candles for lighting. We bought dozens of them, prompted by the fact that there were still wall fittings for candles. These were gold-rimmed white porcelain and they looked especially good against the rose-coloured walls in the dining room.

We were standing in front of the sitting room fire sipping Canadian rye.

"I think someone should be playing a spinet in this room," I said.

"Well, feel free," he said. "What's a spinet?"

"It's a virginal, and we could have someone warbling 'Believe me if all those endearing young charms'."

"Yes, that sounds virginal enough."

"I'd love to know the history of this house," I said.

"I'm sure there aren't any ghosts in it."

"Oh, I don't know about that," I replied.

"That's the Irish in you," Sandy said. "No, the only spirits here are in these glasses and this is the best drink of the night. Here, before anyone else turns up."

"Yes, it feels like Christmas."

"Happy Christmas, kid," he said, lifting my hand and taking a sip from my glass. I laughed because he sounded like

Humphrey Bogart. Yes, he looked a little like him too, or would in a few years from now.

It promised to be a great party. Everyone came, including the neighbours, in case they were disturbed by the noise. They were good fun and added to the happy atmosphere of the night.

By three o'clock in the morning everyone was in the kitchen. Claude Citron, a French-Canadian, lifted me up to sit on the big pine table and asked me to sing 'Lady be good'. Lyn went upstairs I assumed to look for Sandy, who was missing. Did she go for him to hear the song, or did she think Claude was making too much of a fuss of me? It was unusual for Lyn to walk out when I was singing. She was always a fan of mine.

Oh sweet and lovely lady be good,
Lady be good to me.

It was one of the most popular songs at the time and the party all seemed to enjoy it. Claude lifted me down and held me rather longer than was necessary. He attempted to kiss me, cheered on by the others Everybody was cheering and laughing when Sandy came in. We didn't know what Lyn had said, but seeing his expression, Pat O'Connor, another Irish Canadian, caught his arm.

"It's all in fun Sands," he said, but he was shrugged off.

"Sorry Sands, I got carried away," Claude said.

"Go to hell Citron," he yelled. "Just get the hell out of here."

I caught Claude's hand. "He's not going anywhere," I said. "It was the song that caused the trouble. You know it's only a party piece. Where were you anyway? I didn't know you'd gone upstairs."

Maybe I could have been more placatory, but I was annoyed with him for spoiling the night. Anyway, we'd all had enough to drink and it was probably time to go home.

It was not mentioned again. The news the next day put everything else out of our minds.

At four o'clock that morning the Japanese were already on their way to carving another indelible date in the history of the world. It was the 7th December 1941, and their target was Pearl Harbour, Hawaii. That was the day we were to hear of catastrophic losses of men and ships and, a couple of days later, of the sinking of the British battleships *Prince of Wales* and *Repulse* in the Far East. The Japanese were sweeping across the Pacific leaving a trail of destruction behind them.

Just before Christmas I came across a newly produced copy of the *Book of Kells* in Foyle's bookshop on Charing Cross Road. It was lovely, with a white and gold cover and good pictures. I decided to buy it for Sandy. It took all my money, which wasn't saying a lot. I printed the one word MYOSOTIS below the credits, using the same majuscule script as the book. I didn't want it to be too obvious. 'Forget-me-not'; it wasn't a lot to ask.

In the evening Sandy telephoned asking me to meet him at the Nelson, another of our local pubs. I wrapped the book and walked up the road. I was shocked by his cold greeting.

"I didn't know you were meeting Claude Citron," he said.

"What are you talking about?" I said rather feebly, upset by his manner.

"He told someone he was taking you to the theatre."

"It's the first I've heard of it. Who did he tell?"

"No one you know, but I know you didn't object to his kisses at the party."

"Believe it or not, I never kissed him, and I'm not going to the theatre with him." Claude had made several attempts to kiss me, urged on by the others but, although we were both willing, it didn't actually happen. The flesh was willing, you could say, but the spirit was reluctant. We got so close, only to come up against a powerful resistance. "Sandy'll kill me," he had said, and pulled back, however reluctantly.

Sandy was calming down, but I was annoyed with him.

"God, I'm becoming paranoid," he said. "I'm sorry I upset you. May I come back with you?"

"Not tonight," I said and, getting up to go, I left the book in front of him. "Happy Christmas," I said.

He followed me out into the street. "Let me come back with you," he said. I felt I should resist, but I could never remain cross for long. I caught his hand and we walked down the road.

Chapter 7 - 1941

On Christmas Day came the news of the surrender of Hong Kong and the capture of thousands of British servicemen, and, as the year ended we heard that the Russian winter was taking its toll on the German army as it had on Napoleon's in another war, but in besieged Leningrad the people were dying in thousands from cold and starvation.

A Nightingale Sang

Chapter 8

1942

Half-way through January 1942, the first contingent of American troops arrived in Britain. The G.Is had landed! G.I. - Government Issue. They christened themselves and we came to wonder how they could have been called anything else. These were the Doughboys. They were good-humoured, generous – and randy, and they were going to give the girls the time of their lives.

They didn't want to be seen anywhere without a girl, not even at a football match. To be seen without a female by their side meant that they couldn't get one, and this was something no self-respecting G.I. would admit to. They were to be seen in every place of entertainment, and they were great dancers – to a man.

We were amused at their rather appealing way of apologising for not using a knife except to cut their food. Apparently, among the things they had been told about the British before they left the United States, was that they should train themselves to use a knife and fork together at dinner, instead of cutting the food first and then using only the fork. I'm sure we wouldn't have noticed the difference if they hadn't drawn our attention to it. They had all sorts of instructions before they landed in Britain, including the risks involved in picking up prostitutes, which resulted in a stampede to Piccadilly.

Of course, it wasn't a total success story, more a love/hate affair that would last till the end of the war. Until the last all-clear would sound, British 'other ranks' would resent having to leave their women to the tender mercies of men who, as they said, were 'over-sexed, overpaid and over here'.

For us they made a difference to life in England. Their entertainers followed the troops, bringing the best comedians and musical shows then available. Irving Berlin came over with 'This is the Army'. Tickets were like gold-dust, but Sandy managed to get four, and, to my surprise, Greg Horan joined us with a girl called Jean who described herself as his 'steady'. She was lovely and we all went back to Sandy's for supper. The house was looking more like home with newspapers lying around, and books with an odd assortment of markers, like bus tickets, sticking out of them. We talked well into the night and they almost forgot to go home.

As time went on we were to enjoy so many other American entertainers. Bob Hope was a regular visitor, so were Bing Crosby and Frank Sinatra; and Jo Stafford, Peggy Lee and Dinah Shore became household names. We became familiar with American humour and their singers, and we didn't want any others.

In February, we were shocked to hear that Singapore had fallen. Most of us knew someone there and we worried about them left to the mercy of the Japanese. On top of that, the papers reported that the German ships *Scharnhorst* and *Gneisenau*, as well as the heavy cruiser *Prinz Eugen* had been able to sail up the English Channel under the very noses of the Government, and out into the North Sea.

It took all Winston Churchill's eloquence to reassure his people; to remind them that they were no longer alone. Now they had the two major powers, the United States and Soviet Russia on their side. He reminded them of all they'd been through, and the courage they had shown up to now, and he assured them of his conviction that they would continue to show the same courage to the end.

In the Overseas Club I talked to Australian servicemen on the night after the port of Darwin was bombed by the Japanese and all the ships in the harbour were destroyed. Instead of the usual good humour, I found them very depressed.

"What can we do over here if the Japs land in Australia? They're already within striking distance."

At that time, most of their soldiers were in the Western Desert, defending Tobruk. It was a bad time for them. Rommel had managed to capture Bir Hamein from the Free French before he made another attack on Tobruk on his way to Egypt.

There was a boost for the Americans in the Far East when the four aircraft carriers attacking Midway Island were sunk. It compensated to some extent for Pearl Harbour where all the carriers had been engaged. But for Churchill, Malta was another worry. It was under constant attack and was in danger of capitulating. One of my friends, who was on board the aircraft carrier *Ark Royal*, defending Malta, would tell me later that they had lived on tomatoes for months.

The losses at sea were still the major cause for worry. During February, sixty-five Allied ships were sunk off the brightly-lit east coast of America, and, in March, more ships were sunk than in any month since the beginning of the war.

The cruisers *Cornwall* and *Dorsetshire* were among several ships sunk in the Indian Ocean. The news of the loss of the latter brought gloom to our office. Diana's father was her captain and she was in great distress until she heard that he was safe.

The captain of the *Dorsetshire* was Augustus Agar, an Irishman who had sailed in *Asgard I* with Erskine Childers Senior. Afterwards he was awarded the first Victoria Cross of the First World War. When he eventually got to London, he had an amusing story to tell of a seasoned sailor who had stood beside him on the deck of the *Dorsetshire* when she was going down. He was undressing, ready to swim clear when the time was right but, well trained in naval procedure from boyhood, he was folding each garment carefully and placing them in a neat pile on deck beside him.

Naval officers loved to tell these stories about the old sailors.

At the beginning of March, we heard that the cruiser
Exeter had been sunk by the Japanese in the Java Sea. She
had survived the Battle of the River Plate at Montevideo
where, with *Ajax* and *Achilles*, they had kept the German
battleship *Graf Spee* holed up until her captain had no
alternative but to scuttle her. Afterwards the crews of the three
ships had been honoured with a celebratory march through
London. This made the *Exeter*'s loss all the more poignant for
the people at home.

In April German bombers were carrying out what
became known as the Baedeker Raids on England's
medieval cities, and one of the voluntary workers from our
canteen had gone to the old city of Bath for a rest. She had
been involved in voluntary work throughout the war and she
was tired and looking forward to this short break. Sadly, Bath
was raided on the night she arrived with her daughter and she
was killed. Her husband, who led the band of the Irish Guards,
arrived home to find the table laid for his meal. The sad news
came through from Bath and he found his daughter wounded
in one of the hospitals.

I was feeling that I had to get out of London, even for a
few days. I said so to Sandy.

"Why don't we go to Oxford for the weekend? You like
that place."

"I'd love that," I said. "The place fascinates me. In the
Middle Ages it was like ancient Athens, where people
gathered around the learned men of the time. That was before
the colleges were established.

"The early colleges were monastic schools and they had a large number of Irish students who lived in places called Irisch Streets or Ireland Hill. They had their own Halles Hibernia. Nowadays you're likely to hear that they were a wild lot. Well, they would have been different, I suppose, and misunderstood."

"No doubt," he said wryly.

"We could find a hotel close to the railway station, couldn't we?"

"I think we should walk around for a while until we find a place that we really like," Sandy said. "There must be some very attractive hotels there."

We left London early on the Saturday morning and in Oxford we found a lovely old house overlooking the river, not far from the Botanic Gardens. It was perfect. I wanted to see as much of the place as I could, but when we had visited three or four colleges, Sandy began to look alarmed.

"How many colleges are there?" he asked.

"I think there are about forty," I said. "But it's alright, I've seen enough. I might get a chance to study here after the war."

I wanted to go on talking about my favourite city. "They had a lot of trouble here in the early days between the university and the townspeople who objected to their growing arrogance. Their confrontations became known as the battles of Town and Gown, and on one very serious occasion sixty-five people were killed.

"Trinity College in Dublin had similar problems with the butcher boys from the Ormond Market," I continued.

Sandy listened patiently. It was a lovely day. We found a restaurant which was serving better food than we would normally find in London and we ended the evening in the oldest pub in the city. I was feeling very sentimental by then.

We hadn't looked at a paper while we were away, but we found that the news had not improved.

In Czechoslovakia the SS Chief, Reinhardt Heydrich, died of wounds which had been inflicted by Czech patriots, and on the day he was buried in early June, all the men in the village of Lidice were rounded up and shot. The women and children were sent to Auschwitz and killed there.

Later in the month, thirty thousand men surrendered to Rommel at Tobruk. This was terrible news for Churchill and for the people, but, with unstinted help from the United States, British and Commonwealth troops did manage to halt Rommel at El Alamein, uncomfortably close to Alexandria. It became vital for them to hold El Alamein.

At the end of July, I went to Ireland for my annual holiday. It was wonderful to be home with the family. No one who hadn't been through it could realise what a haven Ireland was after London at that time. After untroubled nights I would wake up to the sound of the sea lapping against the tide wall, then I would have really good food and had my mother to myself when they had all gone out in the morning. That used to be the time of day during the school holidays when she taught me all the songs I wanted to learn, but now it was the time when I realised there were things I couldn't tell her.

I had never told my parents that I had been hurt in an air raid. During the six weeks I had been in hospital I had sent my letters back to London to be posted there. My sweet gentle father had woken up one night saying that I was at the door. "Why doesn't someone let Frances in?" he asked. He said he knew that I was in trouble, but my mother was a very happy woman. Everyone sought her company because she made them feel good, but she saw and heard only the things that made her happy, and we played this game with her. We told her what she would like to hear and this worked very well. I said nothing about the hospital now because they would want to keep me at home, and I wanted to go back to Sandy.

Above all now, I didn't want to tell my mother about Sandy. I couldn't tell her that I was going out with a man who was married to someone else; that when the war is over he would be going back to where he belongs and I would be alone.

Yes, it was in Rosbeg that the reality of the whole situation hit home. I would have to talk to Sandy. When I got back I would tell him that it couldn't go on, we would have to make a break.

It didn't happen. When Sandy met me at Euston he was quiet and obviously upset.

"Don't go back to Chelsea yet," he said, and we returned instead to the house in South Kensington. I had missed him and I was happy when he put his arms around me inside the door. Still, he was quiet.

"Is something wrong," I asked.

"Yes, we had desperately bad news yesterday. We've lost thousands of men. Of the five thousand Canadians who landed at Dieppe as a rehearsal for an invasion of northern France, a thousand were killed and two thousand were taken prisoner. All their vehicles and equipment had to be abandoned on the beach. The Germans had decoded the signals and were waiting for them." The whole sad story came tumbling out.

I listened but said nothing. If the information was to be made public, it would be in the papers. If not, he might regret having said anything. I thought of the warning jingle I passed every morning in the tube station:

If you've news of our munitions
Keep it dark,
Ships or planes or troop positions
Keep it dark.
Lives are lost through conversation,
Here's a tip for the duration,
If you've private information
Keep it dark.

The words were stamped on my memory. I would never forget them.

"Let me get you a drink," I said.

"I'd rather go to bed," he said. "I've missed you so much."

It was not going to be easy to say what I had in mind, and certainly not today.

Chapter 9

1942

I had been back from Ireland for almost a week now and still I'd said nothing to Sandy about how I felt. In fact I was still in South Kensington, although I'd been in touch with Alan Forte who looked after the house in Oakley Street to say that I would be going back there soon. Then, in the middle of one particular busy afternoon, there was a telephone call from Tom. I couldn't believe my ears.

"Where are you?" I said.

"I'm at home at the moment. They've had a shock as well. I can't wait to see you. When can we meet? Its' been such an age, Frances. Have you changed? Have I been away too long?"

Oh don't, Tom, I thought. That was not how I wanted it to be. Maybe Tom had always loved me in his own sweet way. Certainly he had always supported me in everything and I wished I could fall in love with him, but that was not the way I felt.

"What's happening in the music world," Tom asked to break the awkward silence.

Now I was on safer ground. "It's been pretty good the last couple of months. I saw *Die Fledermaus* recently and at the moment Myra Hess is giving lunchtime recitals in the National Gallery. I go there sometimes. They serve kedgeree and it's not at all bad."

"Sounds good to me," he said, "much better than a seat in the gods at Covent Garden. Do you remember when I used to fold my jacket for you to sit on? Those benches were hard."

"I remember it well," I said, "and I'm dying to see you." It was true. I was dying to see him. He sounded, well, the way Tom had always sounded, sweet and kind.

The following evening, surrounded by the devastation of the bombing raids, we strolled in Battersea Park, enjoying the late sunshine. It was not easy to talk about old times. There was nothing about wartime London which even vaguely resembled the old days. I felt slightly awkward. My life had changed completely. Those simple pre-war days were sort of warm and flat compared with the tumultuous times we'd been living through. I thought we should have a drink. I wanted to relax and to make Tom feel welcome without implying that we could be any more than friends.

We went to the Six Bells in Chelsea. I hadn't told Sandy I'd be late. I didn't want to have to account for my movements.

Tom tried to tell me how he felt being home after such a long time. "They were years of dreaming and longing for family and friends," he said. But he had come back to an alien world and it saddened him. I would like to have been able to comfort him, but it wasn't easy any more. He was almost a stranger – a sad stranger.

To hell with the war! I hate it, I thought. But how much did I hate it? Did I really want that cosy predictable existence now? The war had changed us all. Three years of death and destruction; of losing friends and relatives; of falling in love in highly emotional times. We had all grown up. Life would never be the same.

Tom was ordering a fourth drink, each one different from the one before. "We're out of that". It was always the same now, and we were beginning to feel the effects of whatever ersatz liquor they were serving. I moved a little closer to Tom. Tom was lovely. There would never be anyone nicer than Tom. So why didn't I fall in love with him. Human nature could be perverse. He turned round to face me.

"I love you, Fran. I want to marry you," he said. "The thought of seeing you again was all that made life bearable when I was away."

After his last letter, this shouldn't have been totally unexpected, but I had to search for words. I didn't want to hurt him.

"Give me a little time, Tom. We have to get to know each other again."

"I can wait if there's any hope. I have next Friday evening off and I'm due ten days leave sometime. I'll ring you."

"That will be fine," I said. He called a taxi for me and kissed me goodnight. The earth did not move. Then he rushed for the last train, as we had done so often in the old days.

Sandy was waiting up. "Hey, I was worried about you. Where've you been?"

"I met an old friend."

"You could have called."

"I thought you'd be out. We usually go out on Wednesdays."

"But we'd asked our neighbours round for a drink."

"Oh damn, I'd forgotten that. I'm sorry."

"I know I've no right to be jealous, Fran, but I am, goddammit."

"I love you Sandy, but there's no future for me with you. I don't want to leave you, but I must. The longer I stay, the harder it's going to be. Maybe for you too." The drink was talking. I had not prepared a speech.

"Come here," he said.

"I don't know how I can leave you," I said. "Go to bed and leave me alone for a while." He hesitated. "Really, I need some time."

I slept in the chair.

Sometime later I woke up. Sandy was standing beside me with a hot drink. I took the cup without asking what it was.

"I couldn't sleep," he said. "You can't have meant what you said tonight."

"What else is there," I asked. "How could I face the end of the war. You'll be going back to Canada and your wife when this is over, but even if you didn't I couldn't marry you. I wouldn't marry you." He looked surprised. "You may not believe it, but at the end of the day, I keep the rules. I think I always will."

"Except one," he said, with the same mischievous grin that had been my undoing in the first place.

"Alright, except one," I said. "I wasn't looking very far ahead when I fell in love with you, but the longer I stay with you, the harder it will be to leave. We're coming to the end of the road."

I felt sorry for myself and I cried. He put his arms around me. I don't think it struck me that he might be hurt as well. He was ten years older than me and he was stronger. He'd be alright I felt sure. No, I was just sorry for myself.

"I didn't know how you felt," he said. "I've just let things drift on. It was so good to have you around. We've both had a lot of fun, I think. You've made all the difference to my life in England, but I haven't been fair to you. Even now, I don't want you to go. I'm asking you to stay with me. Six months ago I knew I should let you go, but I backed down. I put it off."

What happened six months ago I found myself wondering. I was in no mood to ask. I'd forgotten about the drink he'd brought. It was cold now.

He kissed me. "Come to bed," he said.

Remembering the reference to "six months ago" the following day, I thought of the Christmas party and Claude Citron and decided that must have been the time.

When Tom rang it was to invite me to lunch with his family on the Sunday.

He met me at the local station and we went for a walk on the Shirley Hills. It was lovely, but there was a high, wind and my long hair was tousled. It was Tom who reminded me to comb it before we got to the house and who smoothed down the bit I had missed at the back. I should have guessed that this visit was important to him.

I was not prepared for the grandeur of Tom's house, nor for his mother's exquisite beauty, and I wished I had taken more care with my appearance.

I guessed that Tom's mother had married twice. There were two young children in the house. They were all charming and later in the day Mrs. Faulkener suggested that I should stay the night instead of going back to London on my own. Tom would be going back to barracks at crack of dawn.

It seemed churlish to refuse, but what was I going to say to Sandy. He was already unhappy about the other night. I couldn't telephone from here so I would have to face that problem tomorrow. I didn't sleep well and I was awake when Tom came in to say goodbye. I could feel his rough uniform and brass buttons through the flimsy nightdress I had borrowed, and I was surprised to find how much I enjoyed his kisses, but my feelings were stillborn when I thought of his parents next door. That was a pity. In other circumstances our friendship might have become a romance.

"I don't' know how much longer we will be in England," Tom said, "but I'll be getting leave before we go. I'll try to get next weekend off anyway Fran and I'll book for the theatre on Friday night. You will come, won't you darling? It will be like old times."

I wish it could be like old times, I thought. It was great having Tom for a friend. I didn't have to think about marriage then. Everything was so complicated now.

"Will you ring me during the week Tom and we can make arrangements?"

"Of course. I'll be looking forward to the weekend."

Tom was shy. It had not been easy for him to ask me to marry him. He needed the few drinks that night. I wondered about marriage with Tom. People did marry their best friends, but I didn't feel that it would work for me.

"Goodbye darling" he said, "see you soon."

Tom's father took me to the station after breakfast. I was glad to go because I was pretty sure they all knew that Tom wanted to marry me and I couldn't cope with that situation at the moment. Leaving Sandy was all I could think of for the time being.

Lyn rang the office during the morning asking me to join her for lunch. It seemed that when I hadn't returned the night before, Sandy had rung Lyn.

"He said he knew things were coming to a head," Lyn said. "What's going on? Where were you last night? Why didn't you telephone? I've never heard Sandy like that before. He'd obviously been drinking. He was really fed up."

Lyn knew that Tom had come home and I told her the rest of the story.

"I know what I'm going to do," I said suddenly. "I'll go home for a while. I'll go as soon as I can get a sailing ticket."

When I got home in the evening, I told Sandy that I was planning to go to Ireland as soon as I could. "I need time to think things over," I said.

"Will you come back?" he asked. He was very quiet.
"I will come back, but not for a while."
"It's all over, isn't it?"
"It could have been forever if you were free," I said.

Draw a veil over yesterday
Adios
Adieu
To God forever,

Chapter 9 - 1942

A last supper
of lobster and wine and Canadian rye,
but goodbye became wait
one more night
just one more night.

Now it was Saturday and Sandy had arranged a swanky dinner at the Ritz, where we both drank a little too much wine. We took a taxi to Euston and arrived long before train time. The station was almost in complete darkness, but we found the platform and chose a carriage. It was all silent and black as the grave. Maybe he hoped we would make love, but I felt drained and numb. I don't know how long we'd been sitting there in silence, holding hands, when he got up and opened the door and, without a word, stepped out and walked back along the deserted platform.

I heard the echo of his footsteps in the silent night, but I didn't look out. I would never see him again.

I sat there stunned. For how long, I don't know, but I found myself thinking of the night he told me he was married. That was when I grew up, I thought, and it hurt, but giving him up would have hurt more, so I didn't. No, I let it go on till I died.

Adios my love. Adieu.
C'est la guerre.

Maybe years from now I'll remember the laughter, forget the tears; remember the love, forget the heartbreak.

A Nightingale Sang

Chapter 10

1942

Now I was alone in the dark. I was stunned. I couldn't believe what had happened. Sandy had gone without saying goodbye. He had left me alone in the dark and I would never see him again. I hadn't even kissed him goodbye. What a way to end our happy love affair. I knew he was hurt and I just felt numb. For the last month I had carried a weight around in my chest that sometimes took my breath away. The only way I could leave Sandy was to let this amnesia set in. It made the parting bearable and I hoped it would last until the pain went away.

When I became aware of the carriage doors banging, I got up and stood in the corridor. The guard was drawing the blinds and turning on the dim lights which they allowed us now, and I didn't want to be found lurking in a dark corner. People were hurrying along the platform and the compartments were beginning to fill up. I took my seat. A young man got in and sat opposite me. He was followed by several others. There was a lot of chatter. Everyone looked happy at the prospect of going home. I closed my eyes, not wanting to be involved.

The train would be overcrowded, as usual these days. Going home from school, I used to have a whole seat to myself where I could stretch out and go to sleep. Nowadays the corridors were crowded. Even the lavatories provided semi-permanent seats for people.

Then, just before we were due to leave, the air raid sirens sounded, followed almost immediately by the sound of gunfire. The guard came along the corridor checking the blackout blinds. Everyone was talking now. People who had travelled from outside London were distinctly uneasy.

"I hope it won't be an all-night affair," someone said.

For an hour we sat in the dimly-lit carriages listening to the distinctive drone of the German planes. Everyone agreed that they sounded different from the British and a silly jingle came into my mind, the sort of thing that we could see all over London these days:

> *'One of ours' said simple Ned*
> *Bombs came down and killed him dead*
> *Then said his wife with laughter merry,*
> *'Ha ha, I knew it was a Jerry'.*

I almost laughed out loud, but the way I was feeling it might sound like hysteria.

The anti-aircraft guns in the distance would be trying to prevent the bombers reaching the built-up areas. No one dared to look out for fear of showing a light. The waiting seemed interminable, but at last there was a lull and, to everyone's relief, the Irish Mail pulled out.

For me it was a nightmare journey. Too much wine at the Ritz, followed by black coffee, had left me with a terrible thirst and there would be no hope of relief until we got to Crewe in the early hours of the morning.

I found the familiar rattle of the train soothing in spite of myself. It reminded me of going home in happier times. But every now and again it would change to a louder forbidding clang which, although I didn't know it at the time, would inspire John B. Keane to write 'Many Young Men of Twenty said Goodbye' at what he described as the loneliest time of his life.

I decided to write a poem to Sandy;

You wore a maple leaf on your shoulder
had a smile like Humphrey Bogart,
we had dinner and we danced,
you were funny and we laughed
and when London town was falling down
you told me not to cry.
You were good to have around.

I gave you a copy of the Book of Kells
and in majuscule script I wrote
one word – 'MYOSOTIS' –
'Forget-me-not' in English.

Now I became aware that people were discussing the war in North Africa; the battle for El Alamein that started when Rommel was on sick leave at home. Montgomery and his troops were particularly well equipped, thanks to America, and they were able to hold El Alamein. They recaptured Tobruk and now it was Rommel's turn to worry. A jubilant Churchill called it 'The end of the beginning'.

It appeared that the husbands of two of the women in the carriage were in North Africa and they were particularly happy about the turn of events there.

I noticed that the young man opposite took no part in the conversation. He had sat with his eyes closed during the air raid and for most of the time afterwards, but when the train stopped at Crewe and I got up to go and get some tea, he said he was going out and would get my tea as well.

There was something dramatic about these blacked-out wartime railway stations. I looked after the man who had just left the carriage. The deep gloom was relieved only by a single light over the tea stall. A rather untidy queue had formed and a woman in a white coat was filling the ubiquitous YMCA mugs from a steaming urn. It looked uninviting, but the tea, bad as it was, helped to relieve my thirst and gave me an opportunity to swallow some codeine. Over the two years that I had endured migraneous headaches, I had tried every available drug. Codeine was the latest and was no more effective than any of the others.

Chapter 10 - 1942

My neighbour told me his name was Frank Durcan and that he was going home to his mother's funeral.

I sympathised with him and realised why he had been looking so sad.

"How far will you be going?" he asked.

"I'm going to Mayo," I said, "to the end of the line – Westport."

"I work for a Mayo man," he said. "He looks after us all very well. We'd do anything for him. My mother felt I was safe as long as I was with Pete."

With thousands of other Irishmen, Frank had been recruited to re-build England's bombed-out towns, roads and airfields. It seemed that neutral Ireland was more useful to England than if she'd been involved in the war. She provided badly needed labour, as well as manning the hospitals and providing about two hundred thousand volunteers for the armed forces into the bargain.

On the other hand, it struck me that Ireland's economic situation would have been disastrous during the war years without the employment provided by her belligerent neighbour.

We boarded the mail boat at about three o'clock in the morning. I took a cabin and managed to sleep until six. I was on deck as we glided by the Kish lightship on a calm sea shortly after dawn. Ever since my first homecoming from school, I felt that I must be up to see that old red hulk. It was my first glimpse of home, and Dun Laoghaire's spires, visible in the grey light, brought back the feeling of childish delight I always experienced coming back.

I took a taxi into the city and had breakfast in a hotel near the station. Since the war started, waiters had taken great delight in giving 'English' visitors enormous helpings and I had to struggle through a meal such as I hadn't seen since my last visit, not wanting to disappoint the waiter.

Due to the shortage of coal, the rest of the journey would be incredibly slow, and there would be no food on the train. Better prepare for the worst. I bought a paper, a magazine and some sandwiches.

I was sitting next to the corridor, watching the passengers boarding the train, when I saw a neighbour from Rosbeg, the brother of the two boys who had gone down on the *Gloucester*. He came in and kissed me, pleased to see someone from home. I sympathised with him over the loss of his brothers.

"It was awful to think that they might have been among the survivors who were machine-gunned as they clung to the wreckage," he said.

"Yes I read about that," I said.

"Didn't you go out with George when you were at school?" he asked.

"No, that was my precocious friend, Margaret. I was the gooseberry and I spent many an uncomfortable hour waiting for her just so that she could tell her parents she was out with me. One day we drove to Cashel in South Connemara with George. We were worried that day because he couldn't resist the Connemara hospitality, and it went on into the night. A gale blew up and it was lashing rain and pitch dark when we left to drive up the rough road across the bog. A couple of feet either way and we'd have been in the mire. Then he got a nose bleed. So he drove the big V8 with one hand and staunched the blood with his handkerchief in the other. It was hair-raising. I don't think we'd have made it but for the cats' eyes. I've never thought of my mother as a worrier, but she was standing at the window that night when we got home."

"George taught us both to drive," I said.

"We used to love to see you two coming home for the holidays. You were like Siamese twins. One was never seen without the other. There you'd be, haring down the hills on those bicycles, long blond hair flying in the wind. You were the studious one."

"Yes, but she could always repair the bikes: fix the chain back on or even mend a puncture, and she could speed through those tricky gates in the demesne."

"Where is she now?" he asked.

"She's in the WAAF, plotting the flight paths of the bombers."

"You should join the WRNS," he said.

"Maybe one day," I said, "if I can tear myself away from London."

"It's great to see you again," he said. "I wish I could offer you some breakfast. I'm starving."

"Oh, I've eaten. Why don't you take these sandwiches. We're bound to be able to pick up something in Athlone. There's always a delay there while Tommy Conlon has a pint."

"Or two," he said. "I can't refuse your offer. I hope I'll be able to get you some lunch."

With Charlie to talk to the time passed very quickly. Like his three brothers, Charlie was in the Navy. Sadly, there were only two left now.

When we got to Athlone, Charlie went in search of some food, but came back with all that was available in the way of nourishment – two bottles of Guinness. I tasted it, but, with the best will in the world, that was as far as I could go.

"I'll tell you what I'll do," he said, "I'll get a bottle of lemonade and you can mix them. That'll do you good."

And so I finished my first bottle of Guinness and, sure enough, it was as good as a meal and kept me going until we got to Westport.

My parents were at the station and Charlie came with us. He lived only a little further out. It was two miles to Rosbeg; two miles to our first sight of the bay. There was a high tide, right up to the sea wall. The old pier was almost covered, but the sturdy wooden bollard rose well out of the water so that the boats could be tied up at any time. I wondered how many generations of our family's boats had held there against the Atlantic gales.

Away out to the horizon the islands looked suspended between the sea and the sky, just as I liked to remember them when I was away. My heart was in this place.

Chapter 10 - 1942

"Beautiful, isn't it," I said to Charlie.
"There's no place like it," he said.

A Nightingale Sang

Chapter 11

1942

Over the next couple of months I had every opportunity to recover my good spirits. It was easier here. I often thought of it as fairyland. Over there was real life. The war was part of another world and Sandy was part of the war. Here in fairyland I could forget, but some days were harder than others.

I woke up one morning feeling hot and headachy. Just another migraine, I thought, but my mother sent for the doctor, suspecting something else. In the middle of the afternoon my friend Grace rushed into the room without ceremony, in a hurry as usual.

"What are you doing in bed?"

"I felt awful this morning. I thought I might be getting the flu, but now I have spots. The doctor's just left. He says it's German measles."

"I don't believe it. I wanted you to meet Jack Conway, a friend of ours who's home on leave from South Africa. I told him you'd go to the dance with him tomorrow night. That's why I'm here now. He's gorgeous and he has only ten days leave. Then he'll be off on the high seas again." She rattled on and I laughed.

"You're crazy. Maybe I wouldn't want to go. Anyway I have the measles, I tell you."

"I wish I was single," she said. She had married at seventeen and she liked to pretend that she regretted it.

"He's a sailor, is he?" I asked.

"Yes he is, and he has only another few days leave so hurry up and get better, will you?"

"Yes, I'll hope to see you before the end of the week, and you'd better go or you'll be getting German measles too."

I was sorry I couldn't go to the dance. It would have been a diversion. I couldn't help wondering what the sailor was like, and now I would never know.

It was several days before I saw Grace again. "Oh, there you are," she said. "I'll ask Jack Conway to come round for a drink this evening."

"I thought he would have gone back by now," I said.

"No, the doctor's given him a certificate, and there's a dance on Friday. It's in Westport House. The new Lord Sligo wants to have more contact with the local people. He won't be spending so much time in London. It will be gorgeous so get out your glad rags. You should wear that white chiffon. You'll take the sight out of his eyes."

"Don't tell me he's been without a girl since he came home. Not from what I've been hearing about him."

"Don't heed them. They haven't a chance."

If you didn't think you were the cat's pyjamas by the time Grace had finished talking, it wasn't her fault.

Chapter 11 - 1942

This should be fun after all, I thought later, when Jack arrived. Grace introduced us and then went down to the kitchen to prepare the drinks. She left the baby, her ten-month old daughter, with us and we talked about the child while we thought about each other.

Jack was tall and well-tanned by the South African sun which showed up his sparking white teeth. I'll bet he looks good in uniform, I thought, but he can't wear that in Ireland, not since the war started anyway.

Grace came back with the drinks and did most of the talking for the next hour, when Jack excused himself and disappeared.

"I told you he'd have a date," I said.

"Oh, that's nothing," she said, and sure enough the next afternoon a small boy arrived at our house with a note from Jack asking if he could take me to the dance.

"Jack said I have to wait," the lad said, and I wrote a note accepting his invitation.

The Marquis of Sligo, who had just come in to his inheritance, was a middle-aged bachelor who had been a member of the famous Cliveden Set which included the playboy Prince of Wales, now banished to the nether regions with his American wife by the British Establishment. We didn't know it then, but his Lordship, who had indulged unwisely during the halcyon days at Cliveden, was now suffering from cirrhosis of the liver. Anyway he was there to greet us and appeared to enjoy the dance as well as the rest of us.

There was plenty of money in Westport House then, but a series of deaths and death duties among the incumbents meant that future holders of the title would have more on their minds than the high life.

"You're as pretty as a picture," Jack said, when I appeared in the white chiffon which Grace recommended. It was great to wear evening dress again and the high-heeled silver shoes which had not seen the nightlight since the first winter of the war. The war? Oh it was a million miles away that night.

There, in 'the castle' on the shores of Clew Bay, where Grainne Uaile, the pirate queen of the west, had seen her grand-daughter married, I fell in love for the last time. Its associations with local history made Westport House a romantic place. There was a full moon and Jack and I walked around the lake getting to know each other.

"Grace says you were in the Spanish Civil War," I said. "How old were you for heaven's sake?"

"That's not strictly true," he said. "I was aboard the light cruiser *Galatea* in Malta as a sixteen-year-old when the fighting broke out in Spain. *Galatea* was the fastest ship in the Med then and we were ordered to sail at top speed for Gibraltar. We completed the thousand miles in thirty-three hours and were awarded the Blue Ribband of the Mediterranean. From that time until the spring of 1939 we were in Spanish waters monitoring the war for the government in London. We went home only once, for the coronation of King George VI in 1937."

"I was at school when the Spanish War broke out so I heard only the Catholic point of view, believing that Franco's defeat would be a disaster. You probably saw a different side out there. I began to think of the political angle when a friend of my mother's came back from a visit and told us of the dire poverty of some of the people there and, later, when I realised that it was a training ground for a Fascist war."

"I must admit that it was all a bit of a skylark for us at the time, although our sympathies tended to be with the Government side," he replied. "It was a government elected by the people when all was said and done."

"I don't suppose the big powers cared all that much for the Spanish people. It seemed to be more a test of their own strength. Did you go ashore during the war?" I asked.

"Oh yes, we visited several ports – Valencia, Barcelona, Cartegena, Alicante. We were all over the place – Cadiz and, of course, Palma. Majorca was pro-Franco. We used to take as much food as we could spare when we went ashore because they were severely rationed."

"I believe it was near-starvation for some," I said.

"There was a serious incident when we were in England in 1937. The Spanish Government forces bombed the German battleship *Deutschland* and killed thirty-one of her crew who were sunbathing on the upper deck. We buried them in Gibraltar. Then, in retaliation, the *Deutschland* bombarded the town of Almeria with her eleven-inch guns and a great many people were killed. But I don't want to bore you with my stories. I'm sure we can think of something better to do."

"I'm really interested," I said. "We all became interested in the Spanish Civil War. It was the start of my interest in politics. We have a Spanish chap living in the house where I am in Chelsea. He was telling us about Barcelona."

"Yes, the night Barcelona was bombed, we were lying alongside, although we'd been assigned a two-mile limit. That was a bad night. We put up a barrage to keep the bombers out of range. That wouldn't have been allowed either, but it was defensive. Hundreds of people were killed.

"I remember there was an Irish ship anchored close to us that night. She had the green, white and orange flag painted on her hull.

"Following that raid, we took a shipload of women and children and old men to Marseilles, and that night we ran into the worst storm I ever remember at sea. They talk about the Bay of Biscay and the Atlantic, but believe me, the Mediterranean can be just as bad. The children were alright. We put them to bed in the mens' hammocks and they slept through the storm, but the old people were in a desperate state. It was pitiful and we were glad to see the warm welcome they got in Marseilles in the morning."

Chapter 11 - 1942

"It was a bitter fight, like all civil wars," I said.

"We sailed on to Cartagena and, by a stroke of luck, the Spanish cruiser *Jamie I* was at anchor there with the senior Spanish admiral on board. When our Commander-in-Chief, Rear Admiral Somerville, heard this, he decided on a bluff. Dressed in his tropical white, lavishly embellished with gold braid, he ordered the galley to be lowered. He had six of his finest able seamen standing up in the boat performing the ceremonial one-two-three stroke in perfect tempo rowing him across to the Spanish ship. The ceremony was completed when they upended their oars and crossed blades in the boat. I wish I'd had a movie camera. He was the consummate showman.

"Sure enough, an hour later he returned with a document of non-intervention signed by the Spanish admiral.

"British shipping had been harassed since the war started and now there was a document promising that they would be able to sail in peace. Somerville was promoted to Vice-Admiral.

"We all knew of one man who would be grateful to Admiral Somerville. That was the Welsh skipper 'Potato Jones'. He had been supplying the hungry Spanish with food since the war started and he had been threatened with dire consequences if he didn't give up. Of course he was a hero with the Government side because they got all his food."

"I suppose the girls got all the food the sailors could spare," I said.

"We made sure of that," Jack said.

"So it was in Spain you were initiated in the ways of the world, was it?"

"Well, maybe so. The married ladies were lonely, and you might even be able to date a single girl if her mother had seen you at mass."

"It's as good a criterion as any other," I said, "and just as ineffectual. Where were you when this war started?"

"I was in Scapa Flow. I spent the winter of 1939 on the *Bramble* mine-sweeping in the North Sea. She's gone now. Her last signal read 'Am engaging eight-inch cruiser'. That would be a ten thousand-ton ship and 'Bramble' carried one four-inch gun. She was blown to kingdom come. So were the three merchant ships she had gone to defend.

"What about you, what have you been doing?" he asked.

"Oh, I've been in London since the day war was declared, and I'm going back there soon."

"Well, this easy life could become a habit I suppose, but it's safer than London."

"I adore it. I don't know how I'll tear myself away, but I will go. I love London too."

"Maybe there's someone special there?"

"Not any more". I wasn't prepared to talk about Sandy yet. "We'd better go back, Grace'll think we're lost," but he stopped to kiss me.

"Your face is cold and your lips are hot," I said.

"So are yours."

"I'd like to try that again," I said.

We forgot about Grace.

"Will you be in town tomorrow night?" he asked.

"Yes, Grace has asked me to come in. She has some sort of a celebration in mind, I think."

"She has. She mentioned it to me too, so I'll see you then," he said before we parted.

In Grace's house the following night, Jack produced a bottle of navy rum. "I know you like this, Arthur," he said to Grace's husband.

"Oh, we'll all have a drop of that," Arthur said, "and you can tell us about South Africa."

Arthur never tired of hearing of Jack's escapades. I felt that he could live out his fantasies listening to jack without having to face the danger and discomfort of leaving home. It was obvious that he thought a lot about him.

"I'm afraid it was pretty boring after the first few months, but I did enjoy the weather and the tennis. Apart from that we were bored out of our minds and ready for any devilment. It was a relief to them and to us when we finally got a U.K. posting.

"I left Durban on the *Lairds Bay*. She was carrying Italian prisoners-of-war back to Britain, and a good-humoured bunch they were too. On my rounds one night I found one of them on sentry duty, standing in for the guard who was sleeping down below: Unfortunately, '*Lairds Bay*' was torpedoed a few days out of Capetown and all the Italians were lost. I was picked up, and the following week I sailed out of Capetown again on the liner *Osturius*. She was hardly fit for troop-carrying, but luck was with us and we arrived safely in Greenock.

"I arrived with a bout of malaria and I was transferred to hospital in Glasgow."

Jack had only three more days at home. I knew I was going to miss him. We were all going to meet again in Grace's for a final farewell.

I loved Grace's drawing room. It was upstairs overlooking the river and there was plenty of music for Jack's send-off. Grace was a pianist and there were a couple of guitar players. Arthur played the mandolin and everybody sang. It was a bitter sweet night. We were all going to miss this crazy sailor.

> *Beneath the spell of a June night*
> *I met a sailor young and gay,*
> *We fell in love in the moonlight ….*

Wartime songs were so sentimental. At one point in the war even the government intervened to advise songwriters against too much nostalgia, which was having a detrimental effect on the morale of the troops.

I felt very emotional on Jack's last night. It seemed that my life had been a series of goodbyes and every time a part of me died. I was captivated by this sailor and, while he was in danger, the war would be all the more frightening for me.

I consoled myself by writing a poem about my new love:

In 1936, Senoritas in Palma
smiled their invitations
and you went

In Cadiz and Cartegena they held you
*   in their gaze*
*   in their arms*
*   in their beds.*

Love was at a premium when hate was in the air.

Chapter 12

1942

Westport was lonely when Jack went away. I started to think seriously about going back to England. I was just waiting for his letter to let me know where he would be going next. There was always the fear that he would be sent to the Far East and that would probably be for three years.

The letter arrived after a week or so. As yet there were no definite orders, he said, but it was rumoured that they would be on Atlantic convoys again.

"I'm hoping you haven't changed your mind about coming back," he wrote. "With any luck I'll be in England every couple of months, for the time being anyway. I dream about our last night together. I hope you have no regrets.

At home, we knew from the war bulletins that the tide had turned for the Allies in the desert, although the capture of Tunis was still evading them and shipping was still forced to use the long route around the Cape of Good Hope, but a relief convoy had got through to Malta from Egypt. I'd had a letter from my friend on the *Ark Royal* describing the excitement on the island when the ships arrived.

I rang Alan Forte in Chelsea to ask whether he had a room for me.

"You're lucky, Frances," he said. "John Best has been called up and he's leaving this weekend. You know the room, the one above your last one. It's a nice big front room."

"Keep it for me Alan, please," I said. "I'll be leaving here on Monday." I'll have to queue for a sailing ticket in Dun Laoghaire, I thought. Hope I'll be lucky.

My parents were not happy about my decision to go back so close to Christmas. I said I'd spend the last night in town with Grace. I always found it easier to leave from there.

"No, stay here," my mother said. "I feel better when I go into the station." So it was decided. It was the least I could do for them.

The final news of victory in El Alamein came through before I left on the 2nd November. The long, long struggle was over and in the end it was heartbreak for Rommel.

I decided to take the ferry to Liverpool and the transport they provided to Lime Street Station, where Jack could meet me. As it happened I was early and waiting there was not a good idea. There were a lot of GIs around and I was getting pretty mad with the constant 'Hi, Blondie'. Some were more persistent than others and I stood and stamped my foot just as Jack appeared around the bookstall.

"Am I late?" he looked anxious.

"No, I was early and this is not the best place to wait."

"I'm sorry," he said. "Come in here and we'll have a coffee," and he gave me a hug. He enquired for all his friends at home. I still hadn't met his family. "I've booked a room for you," he said.

"Oh, thank you," I said, and, after a long silence, "Am I going to be allowed to share it," he asked. He looked bashful.

"Whose name is it in?" I asked.

"It's in my wife's name. I told the receptionist I hadn't seen her for months, but I still didn't know whether I could get the night off. She felt sorry for me," and we both burst out laughing.

"Well, I haven't a wedding ring, if I'm supposed to be Mrs. Conway," I said.

"I've borrowed one," he said. "It's a bit big I'm afraid." Two of my fingers would have fitted into the ring, and we laughed again.

"I see you have plenty of medal ribbons there," I said. "What are they for?"

"Oh, they're for bravery in the dark," he said, grinning. I might have known I wasn't going to get any information.

We spent the evening with some of Jack's friends and he sang me a love song. 'Maria Elena, you're the answer to my prayer'. He sang a very good love song and I felt sentimental. I was falling in love.

In the bar some Irish sailors were singing the ballad of the Jervis Bay. It was a favourite with Irish sailors everywhere.

'Shall my soul pass through old Ireland', they sang in honour of Captain Fegan, the Tipperary man who had fought one of the most gallant actions of the war to save the convoy of thirty-seven ships. *Jervis Bay* had gone down, a raging inferno from stem to stern.

They were strange times. Everything was exaggerated – the wild gaiety when people were together and the black emptiness of the long enforced separations. I wouldn't forget the night in Liverpool and I knew that Jack would remember it too. He was a gentle and appealing lover and, whatever face he showed to the world, I had never doubted that he could be an emotional and loving man. The war was a long way from our thoughts, but it added another dimension to our love-making. When would I see him again? The thought was always there.

"We should get married," Jack said suddenly at breakfast, smiling as he remembered that only a few months ago in South Africa he and two of his friends had made a solemn vow to remain single.

"Don't be daft," I said, for want of something better to say. I was taken by surprise.

"We'll probably have a chance to go home one of these days and I don't want to sleep in one house while you're in another."

"I'm sure it's not that easy to get married," I said, "but we can find a priest and enquire."

Jack had to be back on the ship in the afternoon so we asked a taxi driver to take us to an R.C. church near the docks. He dropped us at St. Anselm's, which stood alone and grey among the ruins of Liverpool's docklands.

There was no sign of a presbytery so we went in, hoping to find someone inside and, sure enough, there was a priest disappearing through a door from the chancel. We followed.

The priest was a pleasant-looking young man who said his name was O'Connor. The church was another institution in England which would have been sadly depleted without its Irish input.

"What's the hurry?" Father O'Connor asked when he heard what we planned to do. "You'll both need letters from your parish and Frances, you'll need a letter of consent from your parents. Why not wait until after the war? You're both young."

"I could be sent to the Far East at any time," Jack said, "and that could be for three years."

I knew he'd like to discourage us, but didn't want to set himself up as judge and jury. "You haven't known each other long, have you, and three years is a long time to be away. In the meantime, you'll have to see the registrar and give him a definite date. He's a stickler for that, so make it sound good. You'll need a Liverpool address, Frances. You can use this one," and he wrote a note for me. "What can I say to you both?

It's a lifetime commitment, you know that, and these are dangerous times.

"Just a minute, Jack," and they both disappeared into the sacristy. Was he going to make an effort to dissuade him, I wondered, and apparently that was what he did.

"Take care of yourselves and I wish you both luck," the priest said when they came out.

I left him feeling worried. Maybe that's what he had intended. We had known each other such a short time. Did we know each other at all?

I got back to London in time for the first air raids for ages. They were reprisals for the Allied raids on Berlin. I had forgotten how frightening they could be.

It was great to see the girls again, but Cynthia had 'flu and would be unable to do her fire-watching stint the following night. I said I would stand in for her and it turned out to be a busy night, but I found it really exhilarating. At midnight, we were on the roof of the town hall where several incendiary bombs had landed and some fires were starting. One looked as though it would take hold and I was ordered over there. It took a while to get it under control, but I found the whole experience very satisfying and decided that I would volunteer for fire-watching duty the following day. I'd had some training early in the war, but this was the first chance I'd had to put it into practice.

Chapter 12 - 1942

Jack's letter, which arrived a couple of weeks before Christmas, was worrying. He said there was no longer any talk of Atlantic convoys and he had no idea what was going to happen, but he would be in Devonport for Christmas. "Is there any hope of you joining me?" he asked.

I'd been so sure that he would be in Liverpool where I could meet him every few months, and now all the fears about the Far East surfaced again. As well as that, I would have to write to Father O'Connor and the registrar in Liverpool to cancel the arrangements we'd made for our wedding. With the future so uncertain, I felt that I dared not leave it any longer. I wrote to ask Jack what he thought. I would be with him for Christmas, I said, but I wouldn't be able to travel until the 23rd, when I would arrive at three o'clock.

Two days before Christmas I travelled to the West Country. I was excited about seeing Jack again and hoped there would be better news by now, but the young man in naval uniform who approached me at the station was a stranger.

"You must be Frances, Jack's girl," he said. I nodded. My name is Nicholas Clarke. I'm afraid Jack is tied up for the rest of the day, but he'll be able to join us at the hotel this evening. He's booked a room. He asked me to take care of you this afternoon.

"Have you eaten? I thought you might like to see Plymouth Hoe. We can find a restaurant up there."

"It's very kind of you," I said. I was disappointed about Jack. We were going to have very little time together anyway, and now I wouldn't see him until the evening.

"Jack and I were on the *Cheshire* together," Nicholas said. "I hadn't seen him since South Africa until the other night. Then yesterday, when he knew he wouldn't be able to get off today, he asked me to meet you."

Every place was snow-covered, but we spent a pleasant few hours on the Hoe, where Drake is said to have finished his game of bowls before he went to meet the Spanish Armada. From the Hoe we looked down on the Barbican where, Nicholas said, Drake's leading hand had waited with the whaler to take his captain out to his ship. It all came to life up here.

> *If the Dons sight Devon*
> *I'll quit the port of heaven*
> *And drum 'em up the Channel*
> *As we drummed 'em long ago.*

"I learnt that at school," I said to Nick.
"So did I," he said.

We were back in the hotel before six o'clock to meet Jack but, by six-thirty when he hadn't arrived, Nick suggested that we should go to the dockyard gates.

"He wouldn't be late," he said. "There's something wrong."

My heart was in my mouth now. "Jack might be able to get to the dockyard gates if he can't get any further. It's just a chance," Nick said.

There was a policeman on the gates, and he took an envelope from his pocket when he saw us. "Are you Frances Carolan?" he asked me.

"Yes," I said, and he handed me the envelope. I glanced at the note inside. The words were swimming on the page.

"Wait for me," was all I could see.

"He's gone," I said to Nicholas. He put his arm around me.

"I'm sorry," he said. "I know how he feels. It happened to me once when Gwen was waiting ashore. Would a drink help?"

"You're very kind Nick," I said, "but if there's a train leaving for London, I'll take it. I'll have to cancel the hotel room." The thought of spending the night in a strange room was more than I could bear.

"I'll cancel the room," he said, "but you'll be very late getting to London. Are you sure you should go back tonight?"

"Yes, it's the only thing to do. Tomorrow is Christmas Eve so I might as well go back to the others. I can take a taxi to Chelsea."

On the London train, everyone was reading, cocooned in their own little world. I was in a daze. I went out into the corridor and watched the snow-covered fields rushing by. The lump in my throat dissolved and the tears fell. I took a crumpled letter out of my handbag and started writing on the back of the envelope:

Do you remember Liverpool
hours stolen from the war
heaven in the fires of hell.

You were in navy blue
guarding British tramps and trawlers
I was dodging German bombs.

We met outside the war
no bombs, no sneaking U-boats hunting in packs
Only love.

I got to Chelsea in the small hours and slept late. In the evening I rang Lyn and, apparently, got her away from the office party. "What are you doing at home?" she said, and I told her the sad story.

"We've all decided to go to the Strand Palace tonight," she said. "You'll have to come with us. You don't want to be at home feeling miserable. I'll be home soon."

I was in no mood for the Strand Palace, but the thought of being alone was worse, so I dressed up and was ready to leave with everyone else. Lyn's brother, who was on leave, was coming too.

There were five or six of us and we were sitting down no more than ten minutes when a group of American airmen came over and introduced themselves. The one they called Oklahoma sat next to me. Everyone was in high good humour, but I was wary. I had one drink and then told the girls I was going home.

They made some feeble attempts to dissuade me, but they knew how I felt. Oklahoma stood up at the same time.

"I'll come with you," he said.

"No, I'm sorry, but I'm not good company tonight."

"Surely I can see you home," he said.

"No, honestly, it's nothing personal. I'm just feeling low."

"Just my goddarn luck," he said. "Let me get you a cab anyway."

Outside he gave an ear-piercing whistle and a taxi pulled over.

"Thank you, I said. "Merry Christmas."

Sitting back in the gloom by myself I thought, yes Frances, merry Christmas. Dejection enveloped me like a shower of rain.

A Nightingale Sang

Chapter 13

1942-1943

The house was empty when I got home. It was awful. I didn't want to be alone thinking of Jack. The thought that he might be in danger brought on a feeling of near-panic. I decided to get busy. There were presents to be wrapped and clothes to be sorted for the next few days. Cynthia's mother would arrive in the morning to take us both to her home in Surrey for the holiday. She had kindly included me in her party at the last minute.

By the time I had finished it was almost eleven o'clock. There was plenty of time to get ready for midnight mass in the church around the corner in Cheyne Row. I felt better. The others would probably go to a nightclub where the £5 plate of sandwiches would be put on each table. This was the licence for drinking after hours. No one ever ate the sandwiches and they looked as though they were produced night after night. I wasn't sorry to miss it.

There was no sign of the girls when I got back from church so I locked my door and went to bed. The last spate of air raids seemed to be over and, with any luck, nothing should disturb my sleep.

In the morning, I woke Cynthia in time for her mother's arrival. We had a pleasant Christmas. Throughout the war, it always amazed me the way housewives and mothers managed to produce delicious meals for special occasions. Did we take it for granted that they would have done without to make sure that their families and friends would be well fed when the time came? It would take a lot more maturity on our part to be able to appreciate all they did for us, and that would include the fathers who would leave their cars at home for months so that sons on leave would have enough petrol to be able to enjoy themselves.

The Australian naval officer who was billeted on Cynthia's mother, was obviously interested in Cynthia and, before the Christmas holiday was over, he had asked her to marry him. He was due to go abroad before Easter, so the wedding would be in the near future.

We all returned to work on the 27th December, I was working in the Northern Ireland Government Office in Cockspur Street now. The girl at the Government Agency thought this was just the job for an Irish girl and I didn't remind her that they claimed to be British. My colleague, Diana, then asserted her claim to Irish nationality through her father, and got the second vacancy. We were happy there and continued our long walks home on the fine evenings. Diana lived in Sloane Square and I continued my walk down the Kings Road to Oakley Street.

I'd had a food parcel from home for Christmas, so I decided to make a cheese soufflé to share with the girls on our first day back at work. The cheese came from Cynthia's vegetarian ration.

Lyn arrived with unexpected news. She had run into Sandy on her way home.

"He was surprised to hear that you were back from Ireland," she said, "and he wondered whether we would both go to their New Year's Eve party. He's a major now and he shares a house in Chiswick with two of his colleagues. That gorgeous French Canadian is one of them, the one who was getting amorous with you at that other party."

"Oh yes, and you went upstairs and told Sandy. What did you say to him anyway?"

"I told him he'd better come down if he didn't want to lose his girl. Are you coming to the party?"

"No, definitely not, but tell him he'll always have a special place in my memory, and congratulations on his promotion."

Nineteen forty-three … We were now into the fourth year of the war and there was still no sign that it would ever end. Lyn had decided against going to Sandy's party and we all went to the Overseas Club instead. We danced and sang Auld Lang Syne and kissed friends and strangers. And I was sad. Where was Jack, I wondered? Was he kissing a stranger, or was he on the high seas, maybe thinking of me? He worried about what he called the temptations of London and I worried about the hazards he had to face. How little we knew of each other. We had spent such a short time together and he was not normally the type to talk a lot. Yet we had been prepared to marry a few months ago.

Jack had a wild streak I knew, which amused his English friends. They expected that of an Irishman, and it attracted me too. Without a doubt he was courageous and he made me laugh. I would trust him I any physical situation and I could see that the men relied on him too. He had an air of authority and I wondered whether I was prepared to subdue my independent streak. I wasn't prepared to spend my life at battling stations, but it wouldn't always be easy I knew. It was in the lap of the gods now anyway. I didn't even know what part of the world he was in.

The shipping losses were frightening. November had been one of the worst months of the war and Churchill was not prepared to think of an invasion of Europe until the Battle of the Atlantic was won. It was obvious that Stalin was getting impatient with the west. There were more posters than ever urging the government to open the Second Front.

The losses on the Russian front were heart-rending by any standards. Stalin was demanding that Stalingrad was defended to the last Russian, and Hitler had forbidden the Germans to surrender even when their position had become untenable. And so the people died – hundreds of thousands of them.

There were valiant stories of attack and defence throughout the Russian campaign. Even the Italians had their moments of glory. They were rarely praised for their military prowess. Far more often they were compared unfavourably with Imperial Rome. Did they belong to the same race? But one day, on the banks of the Don, they came into their own. It was there that six hundred men of the Savoy Cavalry, armed with sabres, charged a two-thousand strong well-armed Russian unit, and routed them. They needed the romantic occasion, was that all?

The early months of 1943 dragged as I waited for a letter from Jack. Nicholas Clarke had tried to reassure me. There was no chance of Jack being sent to the Far East without warning. He would have had ten days leave, he said, if he was going to be away for years. So where was he?

At the beginning of March, we had more air raids and one of them resulted in a major disaster at Bethnal Green in East London. People crushing into the tube station when the warning sounded, caused someone to stumble – we heard it was a woman carrying a baby. At the back, the crowd kept pushing, knocking more and more people down and, in the end, a hundred and seventy-five people died of suffocation. Stories like that were likely to put people off using the public shelters.

Now we were half-way through March and I hadn't seen Jack for three months, but I came back from work one evening to find that a cable had been pushed under my door. It contained three of the phrases permitted by the War Office which told me very little. He had missed me, he sent all his love and he was writing. 'Letter following', it said, so I would have to be patient, but at least I knew that he was safe somewhere. 'Sans Origine' the cable said, over stamped with OVERSEAS.

"Right," Lyn said that evening, "are you coming out to celebrate?"

I had been a wet blanket, but that night we went to the Overseas Club and danced the night away. That was the night I won the leg competition and we all drank the champagne. An Australian naval lieutenant joined our party.

"You're not English," he said, "let me guess. Swedish? Finnish?" Then he said "Christ, don't tell me the girl's Irish. I've sworn by my dead grandmother that I'd never have anything more to do with Irish women."

He meant it. He left us then and now I would never know what dark deeds had been perpetrated in our name. He was handsome too.

Throughout March we had been reading of an escalation in the U-boat warfare, particularly in what was known as the Black Gap in the Atlantic. This was an area in mid-ocean which was beyond the reach of air cover from either Canada or Britain. In the first three weeks of March, well over a hundred ships were lost. It all increased my anxiety for Jack's safety. I had no idea where the cable had come from, but I was inclined to believe it was from Canada, entirely without reason.

At last Jack's letter arrived. He was heartbroken on the night they left Devonport. "To think that you were out there and I couldn't see you. It was an awful night. I haven't heard from Nick, but I know he would have taken care of you. Did you stay in Devonport? We were ordered out to hunt a German raider which had been playing havoc with shipping in the Atlantic. We were sixty-three days hunting this marauder. That's how we counted it, days and nights that were endless, out of sight of land. We crossed the equator six times and finally made landfall in South Africa."

"I cabled yesterday," Jack wrote, "but I don't know how long we will be here, or when we are likely to get home. It could be a long time. While I'm on watch tonight, you're a world away. Are you hiding from German bombs in a concrete pillbox, or are you sheltering in someone else's arms? Don't tell me. I couldn't bear it. I love you and I want you. I thought of you all the time we were at sea. Wait for me, please."

The letter brought back all of the happy memories of our short time together in Westport; that place that was not part of this world of anxiety and danger. I thought of Liverpool when we were in such a hurry to rush off and get married. I wish we had. Suddenly, I had no doubt that we would do it one day, though heaven only knew when.

In London we were enjoying relative peace again. With Bomber Harris in command, it was the German cities that were now enduring saturation bombing. It would be some time before we realised the extent of their suffering, but Hamburg was being wiped off the map, and Berlin was suffering raids of unbelievable ferocity. The Allies were bombing cities all over Germany now, even as far south as Munich. No place was beyond them anymore.

On this particular evening there was no reason for me to stay out late. Fortunately, I decided to go straight home from work, because I was hardly in the door when there was a telephone call for me from Belfast. But I didn't know anyone from Belfast, I was thinking, when I heard Jack's voice.

"What are you doing in Belfast?" I said, when I had recovered my voice.

"We came in to Derry and now I'm at Sydenham Airport. The pilot of a Stirling bomber is giving me a lift to London, so I should see you in a couple of hours."

Things didn't turn out as we expected, as so often happened in those days. I was waiting for Jack to arrive when the telephone rang again. This time from Lee-on-Solent.

"We couldn't land in London this evening," he said. "We've been diverted to this place. Unfortunately, I won't be able to see you till tomorrow."
"I'll take the day off," I said.
"Will you honey?"
"You bet."
"I wish I was in London tonight," he said.
"I wish you were too," I answered.

Chapter 13 – 1942-1943

"Anyway I should be getting leave after this. Is there any chance of you taking leave as well? We could go to Westport."

"I will get leave, don't worry, just as soon as I know when you're going."

At nine o'clock the next morning, Jack rang to say they had landed at Croyden. "Where do I go from here?" he wanted to know.

He didn't know London very well. He had been in the field gun's crew at Olympia in the summer of 1939 and that was about all.

"Walk down the road to Waddon Station and get a train for Charing Cross. I'll meet you at Queen Eleanor's Cross in the front yard of the station. See you soon."

Jack arrived looking tanned and handsome, with more gold braid than before. It was great to see him again, but I was disappointed when he said he had to be back in Croydon at half past five.

"You haven't even one night," I said.

"Not even one," he said.

I had given up the thought of making lunch for him at home because there was nothing in my cupboard except a tin of pilchards. They were always our stand-by. My meat ration had gone in one meal and there was very little at the fishmongers where I called in the morning. He had some smoked cod, which I disliked, some whale meat and slices of inkfish oozing a black liquid on the slab. It looked anything but appetizing.

I suggested to Jack that we should take a walk in Green Park since it was still early, and then we could have lunch at a little place I liked in Leicester Square.

"I'd rather go to Chelsea," he said. "I'd like to see where you live."

"Well, there's nothing but fish cakes there," I said.

"Fish cakes'll be fine," he said, and that's how I disposed of the pilchards.

"Any word of Nick Clarke?" I asked, but Jack only knew that he had left Devonport after promotion.

"We're pretty casual about writing," he said. "We always think we'll run into each other somewhere, but of course it rarely happens, and quite often we're left wondering whether people are still alive."

"I think women are much better at keeping in touch with their friends," I said.

"Nick was aboard the destroyer *Hardy* when she was sunk in Narvik Sound and her captain, Warburton-Lee, was fatally wounded. Nick managed to get him ashore and laid him down with the dead and dying. The leading seaman next to him, close to death as he was but still with a sense of humour, said, 'The last time I was this close to you, Sir, you took a badge from me'. That was his stripe which would have been awarded for good conduct. That was the time Nick lost his finger. You might have noticed it. He caught it between a heavy chain and the ship's side when she was going down."

"I hope he'll make it through the war," I said. "I liked him."

"He's engaged to a Welsh girl, the sister of one of his friends. She's a lovely girl. She wants to have a chicken farm after the war." Jack laughed. "I can't imagine Nick on a chicken farm, but of course he'll be in the navy for ages yet."

"Will you be going back to Derry?"

"No, I'll be at Sydenham for a while. The Navy is taking over from the RAF there, but, of course, I'll be getting a ship when I get back from leave."

"You'd better give yourself an hour and a half to get back to Croydon," I said. "You could take a taxi to London Bridge. The trains are more frequent from there."

"So we have an hour to say goodbye," he said.

It's always goodbye, I thought as I lay in his arms.
Yes, as far as I could see into the future, it would be goodbye.

A Nightingale Sang

Chapter 14

1943

On the 9th May, 1943, the Axis Forces in North Africa surrendered to General Montgomery.

Montgomery of Moville in County Donegal had arrived in Egypt in August 1942 and had taken over from another Irishman, General Claude Auchinleck, who had managed to hold El Alamein against Rommel, the Desert Fox. I have to admit that I was delighted to absorb any information about Irishmen in the forces. I was proud to read of their gallantry; proud when Churchill told the Commons, "Before El Alamein we never had a victory. After El Alamein we never had a defeat."

Montgomery realized from the start that the British Tommy knew more about the German General Rommel than about any British general. This was a situation he intended to change. He visited every unit and spoke to them man-to-man. His high-pitched voice and the black beret of the Royal Tank Regiment became familiar to them all. He gave them confidence. He was always close to the fighting and they felt he would never squander their lives. He turned the fortunes of the Eighth Army around in North Africa. Churchill summed it up in the House of Commons when he told them, "I have never in my life seen troops march with the style or air of the Desert Army."

It was General Auchinleck, however, who was described as the man who saved the Middle East. When he stopped Rommel at El Alamein, he opened the door for Montgomery's subsequent victories.

Early in the war, Churchill had the idea of forming not only an Irish Brigade, but also an Irish squadron in the Royal Air Force under the Irish fighter ace Brendan (Paddy) Finucane. Finucane was killed and the Irish Squadron never materialised. But the Irish Brigade did, in spite of objections from Prime Minister Andrews of Northern Ireland, and it earned nothing but praise. The London Irish with their distinctive caubeens were a familiar sight on the streets of the capital throughout the war years. They were part of the Irish Brigade and suffered heavy losses in North Africa.

For it's always to be seen
the shamrock and the green
in front of the thin red line.

These lines were written for the Irish Fusiliers, known as the 'Faugh an Ballaghs' ('Clear the Way'), or more often the Faughs (their spelling). The English author, Colin Gunner, wrote in his book 'Front of the Line': "I give my gratitude to God that I was able to march with the Faughs, the finest fighting brigade ever to leave England's shore."

Chapter 14 – 1943

There was said to be great pride in the Irish Brigade and a unique relationship between officers and men. "North and south," it was said, "they were simply proud to be Irish."

Within days of Montgomery's taking over as leader, the German forces in Tunisia had surrendered and a softening-up had begun for the invasion of Sicily. At last there was a tangible feeling of relief on the streets of London.

Jack rang from Belfast to say that he would be going on leave the following week and I arranged to take my holidays at the same time. I was excited about seeing him again and I travelled to Belfast via Heysham instead of my usual Holyhead-Dun Laoghaire route. It was easier to get a sailing ticket that way and it would give me another night with him. Conditions on the ship were even more uncomfortable than the other way, but it didn't matter.

We spent the night in Dublin and caught the one and only train to Westport the next morning. It was great to be home, and to look forward to having Jack with us when we went sailing or climbing, or walking the golden beaches to the north of Killary. We had glorious weather and it should have been a heavenly holiday, but things didn't turn out quite as I had hoped.

Jack had a lot of friends in Westport who were always delighted to see him back. He was an excellent sportsman and was always included in any fixtures they arranged. As far as they were concerned, nothing had changed and the games were followed by all-male evenings in the pub. I was in second place, if that.

In an effort to help, Grace invited us to dinner one evening and I was able to arrange for us to spend the following day fishing in the bay. My father warned us that high tide was at seven o'clock in the morning and he moved the boat from our pier to one further out where we could board later. I knew he wanted to come with us, but I was determined to have Jack to myself for once.

The sun shone from early morning and a fine morning on Clew Bay is the nearest thing to heaven in this world. I wore a light yellow sleeveless dress which went well with the tan I was acquiring. If I couldn't have Jack, I wanted him to know what he was missing. I wasn't going to mention that I hadn't seen much of him. He arrived on time. I was to discover that he did everything on time, and we left Hildebrand's pier with a nice sailing breeze. It was wonderful. Just the quiet lap of the water on the timbers and a priceless view. No one could be unhappy on such a day.

According to legend, there are three hundred and sixty-five islands in Clew Bay. Someone had chosen a familiar number to indicate that there are a great many. Few of them are inhabited, but ahead of us now was Inishraher where Paddy Joyce kept a light burning all night, every night, and many a sailor blessed that light.

We lowered our fishing lines and left them trailing while we sailed around the island, coming back through the rough channel that separated it from Inisheeny. It was there, in the channel, that the fish started to tug and they came as fast as we could haul them in. Three times we came back that way until the box in the bottom of the boat was full of silver bodies.

"When I was a child there were two cottages in Inisheeny," I said to Jack. "We called there once, to the one with a model ship over the front door. I longed to have one like it. I thought then it was an idyllic place to live, but the women felt isolated out here and eventually they moved to the mainland. I suppose it's rough here in the winter. Now there's hardly a trace of the houses. How quickly they're reduced to rubble when there's no one to care for them. I'd like to have lunch on Inisheeny, for old time's sake," I said.

We pulled into the little cove facing the mainland and I unpacked the cold chicken and salad and brown bread which my mother had provided. I had included one of the bottles of Graves which I'd discovered in the village pub the day before. They were half hidden on a shelf just under the ceiling.

"What have you up there?" I asked Peggy who owned the place.

"God, I don't know. They must be there forever," she said.

Her greyhound, Flyer, was lying across a box she wanted to use as a stepladder.

"Get up, Flyer," she said, but the dog was reluctant, showing none of the speed which his name implied, and while Peggy tried to urge him to move, I had a look round the shop for any other treasures which might lie hidden.

There were sugared almonds and buttered brazils and a bottle of Chivas Regal whisky, none of which I had seen since before the war. Peggy was reaching up for the four bottles of Graves.

"How much are they?" I asked her.
"God knows," she said. "I suppose ten shillings is enough for them now."

Half a crown for a bottle of Graves, I thought. I'd better include some of those other treasures as well.

After lunch, Jack and I walked over the hill, past all that was left of the walls which had once housed families and through the patches where they had grown their potatoes and cabbages.

At the back of the hill, we faced the familiar outline of Clare Island several miles away and, beyond it, only the wide ocean on its way to Canada. We made love there, hoping that Saint Patrick on his holy mountain was looking the other way. Now I was back again in the tender trap.

"It's hard to imagine that there's a vicious war going on not too far away," I said.

"It might be closer than you think," Jack said. "I've spent many an anxious moment out there; many a lonely one too, thinking of you and wondering what might be going on in London."

Chapter 14 – 1943

"These are the infamous Western Approaches, aren't they? It all sounds so romantic. No, no, I know it hasn't been any fun and, as if torpedoes aren't bad enough, you can have rotten weather. I've seen many an Atlantic storm. You're definitely a hero, my darling. You're all heroes, and I mean that."

"Come here you," he said. "Would you be able to repeat that performance for Saint Patrick, do you think?"

"I could try," I said, forgetting the aggravation of the past week. I loved this man and nothing was going to change that.

"I was maybe six years old when my father took me sailing on Newport Bay," Jack said. "We caught a couple of dozen mackerel and we made a fire on the shore of Achill Beg and fried some of them for our lunch. I'll never forget that feast.

"We explored the island and then set sail for home. My big moment came when my father put my hands on the tiller and told me to steer for a hill on the shoreline. 'keep her bow pointed in that direction,' he said. 'that's your landmark'.

"It was a magic day for me, especially when he'd tell me I was doing well. After that I wanted nothing but the sea. My grandfather hoped I would take over his farm eventually. All his sons had gone to America and I was sent to live with him and my grandmother, but I hated living in the country. Every chance I got, I'd climb the hill where I could see the boats in Newport Bay. He gave up and let me go back to town. He sold out then and they both followed their sons to Chicago. It must have broken his heart."

That lovely day was the only one I spent with Jack during our leave and I came back from Ireland feeling frustrated. It had been a great holiday in some ways. The weather had been perfect and there had been idyllic days, but I wasn't sure whether I featured in Jack's future plans. It wasn't that he was any less ardent, but he was certainly not prepared to settle down yet.

"I wonder where you'll be going after Devonport," I said one day.

"I don't know," he said, "and that's how I like it."

"I think Father O'Connor was right," I said. "We should forget about getting married until after the war. There's plenty of time."

"Why don't we wait and see where I'll be going after this leave. I don't like the idea of leaving you in London. It wouldn't be fair."

"Yes, we'll wait and see what happens next," I said.

When we got back to London, he wanted to leave a civilian suit in my wardrobe, but I said I thought he should take it with him.

Marriage was not mentioned again during 1943.

Chapter 15

1943

I was desolate when Jack left. The situation in Westport had upset me and I couldn't see it changing. I felt that we should call it a day, but I didn't want to let him go. I was miserable, but I decided to leave the next move to him.

Lyn looked in. "No good moping about it," she said. "Come to the club tonight and we'll have a drink."

We spent the evening with some of the American airmen we'd met before. They were upset about the disappearance of a plane they called 'Lady be Good'. One of the men here was the pilot's brother and he said they had failed to return from a bombing mission although it was known that she had not been shot down. He'd had a cable from home and was left to try and solve the mystery.

"She's disappeared off the face of the earth," he said.

We all knew there had been raids on Sicily prior to what everyone believed would be an invasion, the first landing on the European mainland which had been expected to follow victory in North Africa. We left the men feeling sorry for themselves that night. It didn't make me feel any better, but all was well in the morning when a letter arrived from Jack.

"I'll be going on Atlantic convoys," he wrote, "coming in to Liverpool every few months. I'm hoping I'll be able to see you. I'll be sailing on the *Flint Castle*, one of the corvettes for escort duty in the North Atlantic. She has to be fitted with a new weapon and I'm going to Greenock straight away to do a course on its operation. We should be ready to sail in about a month.

"I hope you'll write, Frances, and that I'll see you again before long. Maybe I'll be able to convince you that I love you."

"Feeling better now?" Lyn said when I told her about the letter. "I knew it would be alright."

There were relentless raids on Germany now. Night and day the industrial Ruhr was being pounded without mercy. Guy Gibson had just made the famous 'bouncing bomb' attack on the dams which had caused severe flooding in the Ruhr Valley.

There was good news about the Battle of the Atlantic which was now favouring the Allies. So many U-boats had been sunk during May in this most dangerous war zone that now, at last, we could begin go see the end of the war at sea.

Everyone was talking about the raid on the dams and the men they now called the *Dambusters*, but Guy Gibson called it "sinister and unnerving." From what we read in the papers, they'd had to fly low over the rivers and drop the bombs at precisely the right point, where they would hit and bounce and hit again. Gibson was awarded the Victoria Cross. He survived the raid, but not for very long. Airmen had the shortest life expectancy of all the servicemen.

At the Overseas Club I had agreed to meet one of the American boys for dinner at the Mirabelle the following evening. I liked that place. It was stylish and I was glad I had brought a few new dresses from Westport. I wore a flimsy jacket for the simple reason that I thought I looked good in it and not because it kept me warm on what turned out to be a chilly evening.

"You British girls are tough," my date said. His first name was Du Bois, honestly.

"Irish," I said, "and I'm frozen." He laughed. It was a good start to the evening. We got on well. He had been in England less than a month and he'd got married during his embarkation leave. He said there was not one unmarried man on the ship coming over.

"And I'll bet a lot of them are not going to admit to being married," I said.

"I met my wife only two weeks before our wedding. She's just eighteen and her father refused point blank to give his consent until her mother threatened to come across the State line with us, where we could be married without his consent."

I thought it was crazy, but I wished him luck anyway. Hadn't I almost done the same thing myself not all that long ago. DuBois was stationed in Suffolk and I agreed to meet him whenever he was in town. We were to become good friends. He reminded me a little of Tom. And thinking of Tom, I remembered that I hadn't heard from him for ages. He had been posted abroad when I was in Ireland in 1942. I must write to him, I thought.

How life had changed since the days when Tom and I were at college together. If we had wanted to we could have followed developments in Europe leading up to 1939, but we were all quite determined to ignore the fact that Europe would go to war. We didn't know the extent to which persecution of the Jews had gone, but we weren't unaware of it either and it's hard to believe that the German people were. Whatever else happened, we convinced ourselves that the Great War had to be the last time such a conflict would be imposed upon the world.

The Allies had started to bomb Italian towns now, so it was no big surprise when Churchill broadcast at the end of June 1943 that they were preparing for an assault on Italy, although he was not, of course, prepared to say where it would strike. For people who'd had friends and family in the Desert campaign, that meant more worry.

We didn't have long to wait for the news. On the 10th July, Allied forces landed on the coast of Sicily, backed by a massive naval bombardment. Here was the first offensive on mainland Europe since 1940. This was a blow at the 'soft belly' as the Prime Minister called it, but we all felt now that it was only a matter of time until the main front was opened, and that would be across the English Channel.

Syracuse was occupied by Allied forces on the first night in Sicily, and Palermo was taken later in the week.

At home isolated raids continued and about two hundred people were killed during June. One night we heard that the American Embassy in Grosvenor Square had been hit and four of us set off to walk across Hyde Park, for want of something better to do. It was a big adventure. We joined the huge crowd in Grosvenor Square where the embassy was in flames and soldiers were throwing sacks of records out of upper storey windows. They were yelling, "Come on over here G.I.s. You're needed bad," but, as far as we could see, there was no one rushing in that direction. Were they heeding the old warning 'Never volunteer for anything in the army'?

We were kept away from the building by soldiers with bayonets. We had marched across the park, both ways, singing, with not a care in the world that night, so it was chastening to read in the morning papers that Hyde Park was closed temporarily because of unexploded bombs.

It was during July that Hamburg suffered the first of what were called the Gomorrah Raids. Two and a half thousand people were killed the first night. But four days later, in a raid lasting no more than three-quarters of an hour, the whole centre of the city was turned into a raging inferno which mesmerised and horrified even the men who had caused it.

Only those who could immerse themselves totally in water had any hope of escaping. Spontaneous combustion caused by the fires of hell reduced people to ashes. It was a diabolical act of retaliation.

July was almost over when Jack rang from Liverpool. There was an upheaval in the pit of my stomach when I heard his voice, all the doubts forgotten. Now I wanted nothing more in the world than to see him again.

"How was the trip," I asked.

"Pretty uneventful," he said. I wasn't expecting much information. "Has London been quiet?"

"Not too bad. When did you come in?"

"We tied up a couple of hours ago. Will you be able to come up here? We have two more days. There's a train arriving from Euston at twelve o'clock tomorrow."

"I'll be on that train," I said. I rang Diana to say that I was going to have a migraine for two days. She would pass on the message.

Jack was standing at the barrier, beaming, as I came through.

I was feeling ridiculously happy.

"I refused to play in the cricket match this afternoon," he said, after our greeting.

"I don't believe it."

"Honestly," he said, "do you want to watch it?"

"What time's the next train back?" I said.

"No, I've booked us into a hotel in Southport, away from them all. It's as far as we can go when we have so little time. I hope you'll like it. It's been recommended to me."

"I'd like Bootle if you were there," I said.

"I'm afraid they've bombed poor old Bootle off the map," he said.

Walking on the promenade overlooking the Irish Sea in Southport, I was asking him about the trip to Newfoundland and how he found life on the new ship.

"Our captain is one of the Sitwells," Jack said. "He's a grand fellow, but he's no sailor. On our way to Reykjavik we came across an Icelandic trawler which had broken down and was drifting the North Atlantic. We had to take her in tow and that meant firing a towline on to her deck.

"The line is attached to a short brass rod which is inserted into the barrel of the gun to be fired. It meant coming close to the trawler in the high wind. It was a comedy, I'm telling you.

"You'll have to come in closer," I said to the captain, "and he did. Doing about twenty knots he bore down on the unfortunate vessel, missing her by inches. I've never seen anyone disappear as fast as the fishermen who were waiting to take the line. They must have thought their last hour had come. I'm sure they wonder how we expect to win the war. We often wonder ourselves."

In the evening, in the hotel bar, I sat close to Jack wanting to touch him after so long. We were going to have such a short time together. I wanted it to be the best yet. Any time we had together was special. He could go on talking, or be silent. I didn't care as long as he was there. How could there ever be anyone else.

We had two wonderful nights and of course I wished it could be forever. Jack was probably more practical. I'm sure he didn't daydream like I did, but I know that all the servicemen longed for these special times with girlfriends and families. They kept them human, Jack said.

Now he had to be back on the ship by eight o'clock the following morning. The convoy to St. John's, Newfoundland would sail on the tide. At least I felt now that, although the Atlantic would continue to be fraught with danger, it was not the one-sided battle that it had been during the previous years.

In July, the Prime Minister was able to announce that eighty U-boats had been sunk in recent months.

It was a bleak and lonely world when I left Jack in Liverpool that Friday morning. I was in no mood to chatter on the train and was glad that my fellow passengers were equally unsociable. I had promised to meet Du Bois, whom I now knew as Du, in the evening and although it wouldn't make up for Jack's absence, he was always pleasant company. I would not have wanted to spend the evening alone. It was always a worry when Jack was at sea, but none of us could complain about our social life during the war. We may not always have had the company we particularly wanted, but there was never any need to be alone and, of course, this was one of the things that concerned Jack. Like his friends, he found it hard to believe that he could trust the lucky guys who were left in London. He didn't have to worry.

I spent the evening with Du in the Lord Nelson on the Kings Road, sipping whatever liquor was available. We might start off with the drink we wanted, but by the next one we knew we were going to be told 'we're out of that', and we accepted whatever they had to offer. We had become complacent about what there was to drink. I never enquired where Du stayed in London. I knew he would have come up with other member of his crew and I assumed they had their favourite hotel. Bloomsbury was popular with the Americans.

When I got home, there was music coming from Cynthia's room, so I called in.

"Oh, I wondered where you were," she said. "I knew you expected to come home tonight and I called earlier to know whether you would be interested in a new job."

I wasn't expecting this turn of events. "What is it?" I asked.

She mentioned a well-known London bandleader. "He is looking for a secretary and you're the only one I know who would be free to take the job. I have to stick to my reserved occupation, but you've been out of the country lately, so you're a free agent at the moment, aren't you?"

"I believe that's the case, but I'm happy at the Northern Ireland Government. The pay is the only snag. Money is not high on my list of priorities, but even I find it abysmal."

"Well, think about it and let me know so that I can tell him. He'll be paying double what you get now."

I went off to consider her proposal. Here was one of the best-known bandleaders in London and I would have to admit that the extra money would be useful. I'd be crazy not to go for that. In the morning, I'd ask Cynthia to make an appointment for me to meet him.

The interview went well, and halfway through August I started work in my new job. Jack would be pleased. Music was their life-line on board ship. The radio meant a lot to them and this band was a regular on the airwaves.

Personally, I loved to dance and sing, and I liked my music live. If I heard dance music, I wanted to dance. I wouldn't be likely to sit and listen to it, but that would be part of my new job, timing each tune to make sure they didn't overrun the half-hour slot assigned to them by the BBC.

On my first day, I took a taxi to Rainbow Corner, the American Forces Social Club in Coventry Street, to deliver some music for the dance that evening.

Chapter 15 – 1943

"Call the Ministry on your way back, will you Frances? Go on your knees to them, to make sure I get that extra petrol ration," my new boss said.

"I'll do that," I said. So what if a Spitfire fails to take off for want of fuel, I thought, exaggerating the situation out of all proportion, but I found it hard to take this sort of thing seriously at that time.

As the weeks passed, I came to like the singers and the musicians. The Irish tenor was the most popular member of the band with the public and, for that reason the leader was prepared to put up with his often contentious behaviour. He was known to travel with a lion cub to ensure that he got a compartment to himself, and we were likely to hear parting shots like "when are ye going to give us back the North", as he went on the stage. But he could sing.

A Nightingale Sang

Chapter 16

1943

When the Allies invaded Sicily in July 1943, Montgomery demanded to be the Supreme Commander, while the Americans guarded his left flank. The subordinate role had not suited General Patton, who was always impatient with Montgomery's slow deliberate tactics. Patton steamed ahead around the island and when Montgomery entered Messina with all pomp and circumstance on the 16th August, he can hardly have been happy to have been greeted by the Americans who had arrived the day before.

"What delayed you tourists?" they asked. It was an embarrassing anti-climax.

Italian cities were already suffering heavy Allied air raids, so we knew it was only a matter of time before the troops on Sicily invaded the Italian mainland. This was not going to be a walk-over because, although the Italians couldn't resist, the German troops who had evacuated Sicily, had crossed the Straits of Messina to Salerno and were waiting for the Allied invasion.

On the 13th August, the Allies bombed Rome for a second time and, on the 14th, it was declared an Open City to save it from further destruction. Then, on the 3rd September, four long years after the war had started, Montgomery crossed the Straits of Messina with the Eight Army, to land in Italy. On the afternoon of the same day, Italy signed an armistice with the Allies. In Rome, the Germans disarmed Italian troops and took over the city.

Now all our attention was focused on Italy. Most people had friends or relatives in the Eighth Army and it was exciting to know that they were back on the mainland of Europe for the first time since 1940. They were, we hoped, on their way home.

Throughout the war, London was the magnet for Allied servicemen on leave, and this had disadvantages. Here were young men, away from home and usually desperately wanting women's company, so to avoid embarrassing and sometimes dangerous encounters, girls didn't go home alone at night. Living in town, we used the taxis more often than not, and girls from the suburbs caught the last train home – always the last train. That way, there was always female company and as many girls as possible would crowd into the Ladies Only compartments. Most people kept the rules and, considering the circumstances, not many serious incidents were reported.

On the plus side, there was a great social life. It's no exaggeration to say that it couldn't have been better. Girls have probably never been so spoilt, although, for many, there were long periods of separation from husbands and lovers, and a lot of loneliness. I was very often lonely during the last three years of the war.

The 13th October, 1943, the day Jack expected to be back in Liverpool, was the day Italy declared war on Germany. Now we were to read that Italian soldiers had joined Allied troops in their advance on Rome. But there was no news from Jack, either that day or the next. When there were delays like that, it was easy to believe that something had happened; it was all too easy to worry. However, to my intense relief, there was a telephone call the following night.

As usual, Jack was in high spirits.

"Hello Gorgeous! We've just docked. Will you be able to get up here. We have another two days, same as last time."
I'll catch that early train again, getting in at twelve," I said. I would have to ask for a couple of days leave. I could ring the office from Liverpool. Joe Loss isn't going to be too pleased, I thought.

"You're late coming in, aren't you? I said to Jack. "What happened?"
"I'll tell you when I see you. Will you go straight to the hotel, love? I'll get there as soon as I can."

I was up before dawn to catch the early train from Euston and I was welcomed by the receptionist at the 'Royal George'. Jack had become her favourite man because he had brought her some cigarettes on our last visit. She looked forward to seeing him again and he didn't disappoint her. She told us where everything was happening and we decided to dance in the hotel that evening.

"What was the delay?" I wanted to know.

"Oh, we were hardly out of St. Johns when we ran into a hell of a storm. The older ships weren't able to make any headway and the convoy was ordered to heave to and ride it out. It meant notifying every ship in the convoy and we couldn't use the radio for fear of having the messages intercepted. We had to use the same method as with the Icelandic trawler, with the messages attached to the brass rods in waterproof containers. But the storm force winds meant getting dangerously close to our targets. You could see the rod being carried away by the wind. It was murder and it took ages to notify them all.

We were sitting ducks for the U-boats for two days if only they'd known. It was a relief to get underway again.

"Life on the ocean wave," I said. "Who'd have it? It's bad enough having U-boats to contend with, without having rotten weather."

"They give us hard-lying money on the small ships," he said, but personally I prefer the way they crash into the troughs to the slow heavy roll of the big ships. I don't mind the corvette."

I couldn't remember ever having heard him say anything against the service. I had to accept that he was a born serviceman.

"Good luck to you anyway," I said. "You have my prayers."

"What more could I want?" he said. "How's the job going?"

"O.K., if I still have it, having gone AWOL."

"I heard that band at a dance once in Greene's Playhouse in Glasgow."

"Yes, he's king in Glasgow, I believe. We'll be in Greene's again in a couple of months."

"I remember it well," Jack said. "A local band played for the early part of the dance and then this great Glen Miller sound came from behind a curtain at the far end of the hall – 'In the Mood'. Everyone rushed towards the music. The girls were squealing. That didn't start with Frank Sinatra. A thousand Scottish lassies set the ball rolling. The men were propelled bodily across the floor. Is his Irish tenor still with him?" he asked.

"Oh yes". I told him about the continuing battle over Ireland's rights and wrongs, but Jack had no interest in politics.

"I don't know what's wrong with them," he said. "I've been in action with them all – English, Irish, Scots and Welsh, and I couldn't see any difference in any of them. I've never found any man wanting, however tough the circumstances."

"If it was left to the people, we'd be alright" I said and I said no more, not wishing to disturb my grandfather in his Fenian heaven.

"They love that guy in Scotland," Jack said. No one dances when he sings." As an afterthought, he added, "I hope you won't be in trouble for absconding."

"Nothing could have kept me away," I said.

"Come here," he said.
"Aren't we going to the dance?"
"What dance?" he said.

Jack had all the next day off and we decided to visit Chester, the fortress that defended Roman England from the marauding Welsh. Jack didn't share my interest in history, but he enjoyed our romantic dinner in one of the oldest restaurants in the City, all dark oak panelling and brass wall lights. It made for a very intimate atmosphere. I was crazy about him and would have suffered a wartime cheese sandwich if I could have shared it with him, but tonight was special, our last one together before we faced the unknown again.

When the music started, we danced in a quiet corner and were still holding each other long after the band stopped playing. I wished it could have been forever.

We returned to Liverpool and the 'George' and went to collect our key from the receptionist.
"You two should get married," she said, and we all laughed. Weren't we down in the book as Jack and Frances Conway?"

The next morning I decided to leave the hotel at 6a.m with Jack. I couldn't bear to be left there alone. I would chance getting an early train and arriving at the office before noon.

"There's one just leaving," the ticket collector said and I made a dash for the London platform. The train was crowded.

I squeezed in between the soldiers and their kitbags in the corridor.

"Oi Oi," someone shouted, "this is the prettiest soldier we've seen today. Where's your rifle Tommie?"

I steeled myself against the banter, but a firm voice said, "Lay off lads". It was the sergeant.
"No offence, miss," one man said.
"Not at all," I said. "Could I have a corner of that rail?"
"Could she have a corner of the rail?" There was a yell and an exaggerated push in all directions to leave a space in the middle. Then the compartment door slid open. "There's a seat in here, miss," said a soldier.
Oh my God, I thought. This looks even more intimidating. I was wishing I'd brought a book.
"What has you up so early?" the man asked.
"I have to get back to work. Are you all going to London?"
"Yeah, it's non-stop." I hadn't bothered to ask. "We're going on to Caterham for a transfer abroad. Italy I suppose. Can't stand the Eyeties, me," he said. "Do you live in London?"
"I do."
"I was born in the Big Smoke – Harlesden, but I can't stand it now. I married a Lancashire lass and I'll be living up there after the war. Nice people up there. Are you a Londoner born?"
"No, I'm Irish."
"Lo' of you Irish over here, aren't there?"

"Yes, there are thousands of Irish in the forces," I said, deliberately misinterpreting his question."

"Oh, they're alright I suppose, the Paddies, when you know 'em. The Welsh I can't stand."

"I think they're lovely," I said.

"Wot, the Welsh? All chapel and choirs if you ask me, and that accent, Gawd Almighty."

"Not like the Londoners," I said.

"Now you're takin' the mick, aren't you?"

"As if I would."

He laughed then. "So wot's this job 'as you up before your breakfast?"

"I work for a dance band," I said, naming the band.

"Ya don't, do ya? Wot's 'e like?"

"O.K. when you know him, like the Paddies."

"you're worse than my missus for teasin', you are. You don't look Ahrish, do ya?"

"Why, no shamrock in my ears?"

"You know wha' I mean."

"No".

"Why don't you shut up while you're ahead, Thomson?" someone else said.

"Oh, awright, I was only sayin'".

"Well don't."

Silence followed while Thomson licked his wounds. The green fields had given way to housing. He had helped to pass the time. We were almost in London.

"I didn't mean nothing wrong," the soldier said to me then.

"Of course you didn't, I said. "Don't give it another thought. I won't. Look after yourself and come home safely."

"I'll do me best," he said, "but I can't stand them Eyetalians."

We both laughed at that and I turned to go.

"Would you give us a kiss before you go miss," he said.

"That's for luck Tommie," I said, giving him a peck on the cheek.

"Goodbye miss," he said. It was obvious Thomson didn't want to go to war, and who could blame him?

Back in Chelsea, I thought of Jack:

Hard lying in Atlantic gales
Secret messages from ship to ship
Sick men to board the sickmen's vessel
overcrowded with the wounded
from a killing night on a killing ocean.

No rest for Jack on the corvette.

A Nightingale Sang

Chapter 17

1943

Jack had only been gone a few days when the papers reported the loss of the light cruiser Charybdis with four hundred men. Several bodies were washed up on Channel Island beaches and thousands of the islanders attended their funerals as a protest against the occupying force, although it should be said that the Germans buried them with full military honours.

Shortly after the Charybdis disaster, we read of an attack on the cruiser Aurora. The actor, Kenneth More, was the officer on watch that night and he gave a gruesome description of picking up limbs from the deck with the aid of a torch.

These accounts were unhappy reminders of the dangers the sailors faced every day. Neither was the news coming in from Italy particularly encouraging. The Allies fighting their way up from Palermo were making very slow progress against superior German forces. By the end of October it appeared that they would give up the struggle to reach Rome from the south and, maybe, make another landing closer to the capital.

From the Far East we read that the Burma-Thailand 'Death' Railway was finished at last. The full story of Japanese brutality would be told in time, but even then we knew that thousands of prisoners-of-war died building that line.

In London we were going about our business without too much trouble. The nights were quiet and, in the mornings, Elsie and Doris Waters were on the radio telling anyone who wanted to listen, how to make the best of the dried egg, dried milk and spam which had been added to our diet. It seemed, too, that carrots were in plentiful supply because they were encouraging us to use them in flans and pies, and even jam, pretending they were apples or pears. Most of us had decided by this time what we could tolerate. We didn't expect too much but, as far as I was concerned, rationing and the blackout were the worst part of the war for us in England.

Berlin was suffering much more than London at this stage of the war, with constant saturation bombing. Bomber Harris believed that, if the Americans agreed, they could completely wreck Berlin and, in that way, end the war. Had he forgotten that that was what Hitler had thought about London in 1940? Was Berlin any different? And the loss in Allied aircrews and bombers was insupportable.

By November the Americans had developed the Mustang fighter which could accompany the bombers over Germany, so they were capable of raiding enemy territory during daylight with the protection of their own fighters, their 'little friends'. Now we could read that perhaps twenty German fighters had been shot down in a raid. Day after day now we could see the American Superfortresses flying south over the Thames.

As the years passed, the days of peace became a vague memory, and air raids, blackout, queues, rationing and shortages of all kinds were accepted as normal. However the fear and dread of losing a loved one never lessened. So Jack and I clung to each other and I was devastated when I left him in Liverpool on the Friday morning.

To my great joy, a cable arrived from Jack. I was grateful to the War Office even for the limited messages they allowed.

You are more than ever in my thoughts.
Fondest love. Writing.

At least I knew now that he had reached the other side of the Atlantic safely and I could look forward to receiving a letter in time. He must be feeling homesick, I thought. I had written a letter just after he left, but there was no knowing when he might get it.

Those of us who had taken an interest in the Spanish Civil War and the exploits of their heroine, La Passionaria, regretted to read that her son, Reuben, had been killed in the defence of Stalingrad, but it was good to know that the partisans and Resistance fighters were becoming more active.

Winston Churchill was anxious to enlist the help of the Balkans, where Marshal Tito now had a powerful army under his control. In November, Francois Mitterand had managed to return to France and to organize a new Resistance Committee.

A very passionate letter arrived from Jack, written at three o'clock in the morning when he was on the middle watch:

"In London," he wrote, "it would be impossible for you to imagine the loneliness of a blacked-out ship on this black-hearted ocean full of ghosts, but I hope you will understand how I feel and wait for me.

He was wondering if, somewhere out there, maybe aboard a U-boat, another man was writing a love-letter to a fraulein in blitzed Hamburg or Berlin, and yet was ready, as he was, to release an instrument of death and destruction at a moment's notice.

"What crazy times we live in. Ever since I left Devonport, an excited sixteen-year-old, aboard the *Galatea*, I've been in a war situation.   By now I can't imagine any other. I can only hope that you are safe.   I wouldn't want to come back if you weren't there.

"In case I'm not home for Christmas, you'll know that I'll be thinking of you and wishing I was there."

I read it a dozen times and even had a little weep. Imagine, there are lovers who can be together every night.

That will not be my fate. If I marry Jack we will be apart until we're old. He'll be forty before he leaves the navy. What sort of life can we have then?

To get away from my morbid thoughts, I went up to tell Lyn that I had heard from Jack. Our friends meant so much to us then. We were there for each other through the best and worst times. We were never likely to forget the friends we had made during the war years.

Before I went to bed, I wrote a poem for my love:

Do you hear the win when the night is calm
do you feel the calm in a hurricane
These are the things I wish for you
when you are away and I am alone.

Can you hear my lovesong in the wind
Can you feel my arms around you when it's calm
For the sea and the wind and the silent calm
are with me when you are away.

The raids on Berlin continued. Even on Christmas Eve they were not spared, and over a hundred British airmen were killed that night. On Christmas Day, in an address to the people, President Roosevelt warned that the end was nowhere in sight.

The German pocket battleship *Scharnhorst*, which had been a menace to shipping for so long, was lost on the 26th December. Two thousand of her crew went down, including a contingent of cadets who were aboard for training; a sad Christmas message for many a German home.

There was no word from Jack, which meant that they would be spending the holiday at sea. He would be disappointed, but we were having to travel to Glasgow immediately after Christmas, when the band would be playing at Greene's.

Scotland was lively on New Year's Eve and, with all the work done, I went to the dance. I was jitterbugging with a handsome red-haired Viking, who left me gaping when he said "Cailin deas atá tu" ("you're a pretty girl").

"But you're Danish," I said.

"Yes," he said. "The ship was torpedoed off the West coast of Ireland and I spent several months in hospital in Galway."

"You didn't waste your time," I said.

"My Irish is good?" he asked.

"More Irish than the Irish," I said.

"We Vikings owe you an apology, I believe," he said.

"Well, the Norwegians did more damage than the Danes," I said, "but I'm sure we've forgiven you."

We danced the night away.

Soon it was time to return to London and I picked up a book to read on the train. They were short stories and were reasonably entertaining, but not sufficiently engrossing to keep my mind from wandering.

Chapter 17 – 1943

The 'Ghost Ship' by Richard Middleton put me in mind of my father's phantom ship in Clew Bay. Every now and again, during the last few years before the war, he'd come off the hill behind our house and casually remark that the phantom ship was there again. He would point out the light moving among the islands to us.

"There's no boat due in tonight," was his answer to any doubts we might have.

Now I found myself tying up the story with other events. The handsome young German sea captain who had visited our house and happened to remark that he'd been unable to buy West coast of Ireland charts. He left with some of my father's collection. War would have been the last thing on my father's mind. Hadn't they just been through the 'war to end all wars'?

I remember my brother talking about the German sea scouts who had visited the town; how excited the local company had been, planning activities for them. But the Germans discouraged all their advances and surveyed the area on their own. Then there was Jack's story about the Germans they'd met in Spain during the Civil War, who offered seventy-five pesetas for crisp English pound notes when the Spanish rate was forty.

Did it add up to Hitler's preparation for war? Knowledge of the miles of isolated beaches on Ireland's west coast would have been useful to either side I suppose, but maybe they were just a series of coincidences. We'll never know.

The office was extraordinarily quiet when I got back. I jumped when the postman came in to deliver another batch of fan letters. I always found them rather sad; middle-aged housewives whose biggest thrill was writing love letters to a bandleader known only from his voice on the radio.

I got out a bundle of photographs to send to the fans and I wrote telling them how much their letters meant to their favourite bandleader. It kept the ladies happy I hoped, but did it make me happy? To be honest it gave me little satisfaction and I wondered how long I could go on doing it. One of my friends who was a doctor at the Middlesex Hospital was convinced that I should go in for nursing.

"You should come in to hospital anyway," he said.
"There's bound to be a vacancy," and there was, in the Radiography Department. That's how I left the bandleader and went to work in the Middlesex.

Cynthia's wedding was now arranged for the 23rd January. We were all looking forward to it, but the registry office was fire-bombed on the 21st, the first air raid on London for a long time. About four hundred and fifty planes had come over. The registry office was a sad sight. The ceiling was blackened and still dripping from its drenching by the fire engines. It was a quiet wedding and rather sad, because Paul was going overseas the following day.

Chapter 17 – 1943

I was sad anyway because Jack had already left Liverpool by the time I returned from Scotland. It would be several months before I would see him again.

At the end of January there was another air raid on London. I happened to be alone in the house the following evening, wondering whether I should move my mattress down to the basement again, when the doorbell rang.

A short rather square woman stood there with a small child draped around her neck, his red woolly leggings enveloping her like a thick scarf.

"Oh, I thought it would be Alan. I had rung to say that I was coming with Peter. Is he in?" Her accent was distinctly upper class.

"I'm the only one in the house," I said.

"God damn that man," she said. "I'm Eleanor Palmerston, Alan Forte's wife. How do you do?" None of us had known that Alan was married.

"I'm Frances Carolan." I stood aside to let her in.

"This is Peter," she said. "I'll go and make him some supper." She disappeared in the direction of the basement kitchen. At least now I knew that I didn't have to move my mattress. I could read my book and listen to some music.

The evening passed without any further disturbance. On the nine o'clock news they said the Allies were pinned down at Anzio, where they had landed the week before. They were, apparently, unable to advance in the direction of Rome or link up with those coming from the south.

I made myself some vile dandelion coffee and decided to have a bath and an early night, but when I went to the bathroom, there was the little fellow I had seen at the door, sitting in about four inches of cold water. His big brown eyes opened wide in surprise at the sight of the stranger. He was blue with cold. I picked him up and wrapped him in my towel.

"I like thou," he said, an expression he had picked up in his Quaker nursery, I was to discover. I took him along to my room, wrapped him in a rug and put him in a chair by the fire.

"Where on earth is your mother," I was muttering, when I heard the booming voice, "Peter?"

I opened the door. "He's here," I said.

"Oh, how kind of you. I'd forgotten him. I need looking after, so does Peter. You'll have to come and look after us."

I hoped she was joking.

Chapter 18

1944

The news that the Allies had landed at Anzio had been received with delight by a great many people in Rome. There were about ten thousand partisans in the city, and large numbers of British prisoners-of-war were said to be in hiding there, many of them in the Vatican. They all expected that the troops would be in Rome before the end of January. "They'll be here tomorrow," everyone said, but the days became weeks and the weeks turned to months, and still no Allied soldiers marched down the Via Veneto.

I heard from home that a neighbour's son was missing at Anzio. We knew that thousands had been killed. We realised that things were not going well. They had been digging in when they should have been on the road to Rome, was the opinion of those of us who were home and dry. It would be some time before we knew just how badly they were faring. Ships were being sunk in the harbour, and ashore the soldiers were being wiped out. The Grenadiers had lost almost a whole battalion, and the weather was abominable. The intense cold and the mud everywhere, made it a living hell.

Imagine the feelings of the partisans and the prisoners-of-war when, instead of conquering heroes, the first Allied soldiers to arrive in Rome were prisoners of the Germans, hundreds and hundreds of them.

The Irish Ambassador to the Vatican, Dr. Kiernan, was married to the ballad singer, Delia Murphy. She had a farm outside Rome, and when she went there to get her vegetables, she made a point of taking several Irish priests with her. That they returned wearing army boots under their cassocks appeared to go unnoticed by the Swiss Guards. The diplomatic car was always available when the Allies needed transport, although Dr. Kiernan himself took no part in his wife's activities.

The Irish priest, Monsignor O'Flaherty, helped innumerable prisoners because he was appalled at the Nazi treatment of the Jews, as did several other Irish priests. Fr. O'Flaherty was a great favourite, always ready for a joke and appeared to get great pleasure from his undercover activities, which were all planned from the German college where he lived. He was in constant danger of arrest and was eventually warned not to be seen on the streets of Rome.

In February, the Allies bombed the papal summer residence at Castle Gondolfo, and a few hours later the monastery at Monte Casino was pounded for hours, killing the bishop and two hundred and fifty civilian refugees who were sheltering there. Then Rome, although declared an open city, was bombed twice during March. It was impossible to understand the act of wanton destruction which had reduced the early medieval shrine at Monte Casino to rubble.

In London, Harris decided that the enormous losses of British airmen had become insupportable when four hundred were missing after a raid on Berlin.

The Prime Minister told the House of Commons that thirty-eight thousand aircrew had been lost and ten thousand planes had been destroyed. So many people were affected by the loss of every man.

Air raids on Britain were becoming frequent again. It was noticeable that reinforced concrete buildings withstood the bombing better than the others. Corner houses, often shops or pubs, were generally among the first to go.

My American friend, Du Bois, who was always generous, arrived laden with chocolates, nylons and cosmetics on my birthday. All these luxuries, missing from our lives for so long, were available to the Americans at what they called the PX on their stations. They were greatly appreciated.

We went to see Syd Field in "Strike a New Note'. They were all new performers getting a chance to make their name. A favourite song from the show was *I'm gonna get lit up when the lights go on in London*'. It became very popular during the following year. We enjoyed the lively show and Du left me saying, "I'll see you on Tuesday", as usual, but on Tuesday there was no telephone call, no arrangements to meet anywhere, and I went home early."

I know there was something wrong, but it was a week before I had a letter from one of his friends telling me that his plane had failed to return from a bombing raid on Leipzig. It was terrible news and my thoughts went out to the young girl he had married before he left home. He had talked about her often and their plans for after the war. I couldn't get her out of my mind. I would miss him too. His weekly visit to London had become part of my life.

Now, for the first time in four years, I was in the house almost every night. Lyn had moved to West Kensington and was anxious for me to see her new flat, but for the time being I couldn't be persuaded to make the effort to go over there. Jack was away longer than usual and there was no word from him. I was extremely fearful for him. I had no claim on him and I didn't know his parents. How was I to know if anything happened to him?

The average speed of the convoys was about eight knots, Jack had said. They travelled at the speed of the slowest ship, as we knew.

"I have the greatest respect for the merchant seamen," Jack said once. "Britain couldn't survive without them and some of the ships are potential death traps. The strange thing is they are touchingly grateful to us."

Chapter 18 – 1944

"Only the Queen Mary travels without an escort," he said, "relying on her speed for the safe passage across the Atlantic. She has a destroyer painted on her hull. She passed us once, and from a distance it looks very realistic."

Most of the losses at sea now were on the Russian convoys. The papers had just reported the loss of the British destroyer *Mahratta* in the Barents Sea. All but seventeen of her crew had perished in the icy waters.

The German battleship *Tirpitz* had been operating out of Norway for ages. She was a constant threat to the Russian convoys and, so far, had managed to escape several attempts to destroy her, although she had been damaged by midget submarines on one occasion.

Since the air raids were becoming more frequent, Cynthia and I decided to move our mattresses down to the basement again. There was an 'area' between us and the pavement and it felt safer down there. The big cupboard was still in front of the window to prevent flying glass.

On the Friday night when I was going home from work, I noticed that the butcher had chalked the word 'Offal' on his window. It meant that there was liver available. It was unusual to have any left at this time of day. Normally, it would have been snatched up by housewives earlier in the day. I wasn't all that fond of liver, but beggars can't be choosers and it was better than spam.

I went to the kitchen downstairs to cook my supper, but there was a mouse sitting on the draining board looking up at me. That finished my nights in our home-made shelter next door, with a mattress on the floor. Cynthia preferred mice to bombs so she stayed put.

Lyn rang later. She was feeling sorry for herself. She had boyfriend trouble again and she wanted company.

"Do come over," she said. "You won't have to go back. You can sleep on the sofa," she said. "There's a lovely old pub nearby. That Aubrey Howard is a regular there."

"That's the artist who owns the house where we were going to take a room once, isn't it?" I said.

"That's the one. He wanted you to sit for him."

"I know. That's why I didn't take the room. Lyn, I'll come over this evening, but find another pub. I don't want to see Aubrey Howard. He gives me the creeps."

"O.K. Come over anyway. We'll go somewhere."

In the end we had a pleasant evening by the fire with a couple of bottles of beer and I settled down for the night on the sofa with the only spare blanket in the flat.

I woke up a few hours later to the most infernal din - planes droning, exploding bombs, gunfire and flak clattering on to the road below. I don't think I've ever heard so much noise. This was a seriously heavy raid and it was much too close for comfort.

Lyn came into the room. "Are you cold?" she asked, referring to the one blanket.

Chapter 18 – 1944

"No, I'm shivering but I'm not cold."

We both got a fit of the giggles and couldn't stop. We were nervous. Having woken out of a deep sleep to such concentrated noise was pretty alarming. Lyn was about to make some coffee when was a knock on the door.

"Come on downstairs," her neighbour said, so we dressed quickly and grabbed our coats in case we had to leave the house, and rushed down. They had made tea, but there was no time to drink it. There were further crashes nearby and we watched, fascinated, while a small brown stain slowly spread across the ceiling, getting larger as it went.

"That's my flat, "Lyn yelled suddenly, and we dashed upstairs. It was then she realised that she'd left without her key. She had to borrow a hatchet from her neighbour to break a panel in the door.

There were three incendiary bombs on the floor and the carpet was smouldering. We threw a basin of water over them and Lyn swept them into the dustpan and took them down to the yard. It was like Dante's inferno outside.

The guns were blazing and several fires were out of control. We could hear the constant bells of the ambulances. There were obviously a lot of casualties and the ruins of the big Victorian houses littered the neighbourhood. Dazed and shaken people were standing on the pavement waiting to be taken to hospital.

We went back into the house, wondering whether we should go to a shelter, but we all decided that we would be safer in the basement than on the streets on such a night.

"St. Paul's School is opposite here," one of the girls said. "That's Montgomery's old school and it's generally believed around here that the plans for the invasion are being worked out there. The Germans obviously know more about it than we do. It's six o'clock," the girl Hilary said, "it shouldn't last much longer. Let's have that cup of tea."

Shortly after that all was quiet again and we decided to try and get an hour's sleep. "Otherwise we'll be wrecked," Lyn said, but when I woke again it was ten o'clock.

I called Lyn and rang the office to apologise. They wouldn't have known that the raid was concentrated in our area.
"Come in after lunch," they said.

I returned to South Kensington and walked up from the underground. When I reached the Kings Road, I was surprised to see Pat O'Connor disappearing into a café on the other side of the road. I stood up. Did I want to open up old wounds? I knew that Pat was sharing a house with Sandy and Claude now.

I decided I had to talk to him and followed him in.
"Frances!" he said. "What are you doing here at this time of day?"
"I saw you coming in, I said.

Chapter 18 – 1944

"Have some lunch with me and tell me what you've been doing. You're not at work today?"

I told him about the night with Lyn.

"We heard West Ken got it last night. You were lucky. Where are you spending your evenings when you're not with Lyn? Isn't there a man around?"

"There is a man, but he's not around. He's at sea," I said.

"Oh, a sailor. Are you going to marry him?"

"I will if he asks me again. I don't think he's in any hurry, but then, he's Irish."

"Are you well, honey? You don't put on any weight, do you?"

"Oh, it goes up and down. Six stone sometimes, or 'six rocks' as my American friend used to say."

"Your American friend?"

"I had an American friend. He's missing after a raid on Leipzig. He's officially 'Missing presumed killed'."

"I'm sorry."

"Yes, it's sad. He was a good friend, nothing more, you know. It's lonely without him, but I'm well enough, apart from migraine, and I am in love."

"Sandy's missed you. Nothing's been as much fun."

"Oh, it was good."

"I hope you weren't hurt," he said.

"Well … he helped me to grow up. I left school capable of passing exams but, other than that, a bundle of neuroses. Sex was the major sin. There was no allowance for being in love, nor even for being married, I think, unless you were procreating. He changed my attitude. I believe I'll be a better wife for that."

"I'm sure you'll be great. Unfortunately, we're leaving London any day now. We're going to miss it. God knows what the future holds. We all have great memories of the last four years.

"We certainly have," I said.

"There's been no one else for Sandy."

"Tell him I'll never forget," I said. He kissed me goodbye.

Chapter 19

1944

I arrived at the office shaken by my unexpected meeting with Pat. He thought no one had been hurt, but that was far from the truth. I had told myself it was the time when I'd grown up and it was painful, but I thought it was all over. I had recovered, I thought. Now I wasn't so sure. It had been a particularly bad week – Du's death and Jack's silence, followed by the air raid. These thing would upset anyone, I told myself. But all I could think of now was Sandy going away. It hadn't seemed so bad as long as he was in London.

At the office they were sympathetic about the raid.

"We knew it was West Ken, but of course we didn't know you were there. Go along to the canteen and get a good strong cup of coffee," they said.

"I'm fine now, honestly. I've had lunch and coffee and everything. A night's sleep will put me right again."

A night's sleep! That reminded me of Lyn. I wanted to make sure that she wasn't going back to the flat. I rang as soon as I could.

"You know there's a second divan in my place," I said.

"Thank you Fran, but I'm not moving from here tonight. I'll sleep in the Air Ministry shelter. They're bound to have another go at St. Pauls. I hope our house survives, but I've brought in a suitcase full of the things I treasure in case it goes up in smoke."

"What will you do?"

"One of the girls here had asked me to share with her before I left Chelsea. I'll see her later on."

"Well, you're welcome to my spare bed if you're stuck."

"Thank you, but it should be alright. I don't think Kathy has found anyone yet. She has a big place and her husband is in the army."

"Where is it?"

"Notting Hill Gate."

"Oh, not too far. Anyway, the house hasn't gone yet, but give me a ring if you want me. By the way, I ran into Pat O'Connor this morning."

"Now she tells me."

"He's leaving London. I'll tell you when I see you."

"You alright?" she said.

"Yes, I'm O.K., but it's been quite a week, hasn't it?"

"Come over here for a drink before you go home. I'll meet you at the Strand Palace at six. We can do with one."

Lyn had reason to be grateful for her decision to sleep at the Air Ministry. There was hardly a house left standing on her side of the road that night, but St. Paul's School was still intact. Her neighbours had spent the night with friends. Morbid curiosity took us along there on Saturday afternoon. It was a sad sight. All that remained of the lovely old houses was the rubble that filled the basements. A lot of people had moved out or were in hospital after the first raid, so the death toll was not as high as it might have been. Once again I felt we had somebody's prayers.

On Saturday night, I was amazed to get a telephone call from Jack.

"How are you honey?" he said as if he had seen me yesterday. "Are you going to be able to get leave?"

"Leave? When?"

"Didn't you get my letter?"

"I haven't heard a word since Christmas."

"I posted a letter in Gib telling you that I'd be getting leave after this trip."

"I'm afraid it's at the bottom of the ocean. I can't do anything before Monday now. I'll ask about leave then. I'll have a sob story and I'll get them a good temporary. I have a friend at the Employment Agency so I could be lucky. You'd better go home and I'll do my best to follow."

"What a mess. Do you think you'll manage it? I could come to London."

"From the rumours that are going around, this might be our last chance to get home for a good while. They say that the Government will be stopping all travel out of the country before the invasion starts, and it can't be long now."

"Well, good luck. I'm dying to see you. I hear the raids have started again. Not your way, I hope."

"Not too far away," I said. "I'll see you in a few days, I hope."

Everything worked out as I planned and I boarded the Irish Mail at Euston on Monday night.

There was no sign of Jack at the station when we got to Westport, but my parents were there. I got that familiar feeling of being ten feet tall. I swear I could smell the Atlantic. The air was certainly different. It was great to be home.

Jack arrived out at the house later in the evening and I felt indecently excited. He stayed for a meal and then we walked down to John McBride's for a drink. I held his hand and giggled like a child because I was so happy to be with him again.

"You're a picture," he said, "the way I remember you when I'm away."

There was a great welcome for us. John had recently inherited the pub and fine house from his grandfather who was a brother of the John McBride who was executed in 1916. This had been their family home.

John came over and put his arm around me. "We'll make him jealous," he said. No one would let Jack pay for a drink and, even though it was unusual then for a girl to be seen in a pub in the West, they all appeared to be pleased that I was there.

"I hope I'm going to get a chance to sleep with you," Jack said on the way home.
"I expect we'll find a way," I said. "There's always Inisheeny if the weather warms up a bit," and we laughed at the memory. "We could go to Achill or Clare Island."

Chapter 19 – 1944

"Would you do that?"

"I would if my father would give me the boat. I'll ask him tomorrow."

In the morning I approached him. "Would you mind if Jack and I took the boat for a trip to Achill tomorrow?"

"To Achill!" he said, as if I had suggested going to America. "Does Jack know the bay that well?"

"Of course he does, and I know the channel out to the lighthouse. After that it's plain sailing, isn't it?"

"Jack can be pretty rash you know. I've seen him using full sails when he should have had a couple of reefs in. Does he know that a south-east squall in this bay can whip your sail away?"

"Don't worry darling, I'm a coward even if he's not."

"I would worry. You could get down there and it mightn't be fit to return for days. What would you do then?"

"We'll take no chances, I promise. If it isn't fit to return, we'll stay there."

I felt guilty. Oh hell, we should get married. I don't like this.

"Well, we'll see what the morning is like," he said.

Jack came out early. The morning looked fine to me, but there wasn't a better weatherman around than my father.

"There's nothing good on this day, Frances," he said. I saw my mother's smile. She'd heard it all before.

"Well, how long will it take us? An hour to the lighthouse and another couple of hours to the Sound. It should be alright till then, shouldn't it, even if we have to tack?"

"Yes, three hours should do it, but why do you have to go so far? Island More would be lovely and the Kelly's would be glad to see you. You could stay there if the day turned bad. Many a time I've had to do it." But in the end he gave in. He never refused me anything. He gave Jack strict instructions to take no chances.

I had mixed feelings setting off. I wanted to go with Jack, but I'd like it all to have been above board.

"She's no beauty this one, but she's a great sailing boat," Jack said.

"She's a good girl," I said, stroking her gunwale. I didn't like him running her down. Anyway, how dare he? "I think she's handsome. To me she's the Emerald Gem of the Sea."

"I thought that was Ireland."

"It's this handsome lady as well," I said.

It was a lovely morning with a good steady sailing breeze when we left the pier, but, outside the lighthouse, the wind died completely and we had to use the motor.

"The calm before the storm," I said to Jack.

"Could be," he said. "It seems unnatural."

We were off Achill Beg when there was a sudden squall, "like a shot out of a gun," I'd heard my father say so often. Suddenly, the sea was whipped into a fury and we decided to make for the Sound instead of going round to Keel.

Chapter 19 – 1944

The boat was like a cockle-shell, tossed about by the power of the waves. Jack grabbed the tiller from my hands.

"Go into the cabin," he said. "Good thing we had the sails down."

I was glad of that too. I never liked what my father called 'gybing' and Jack called 'wearing' in a high wind, that is swinging the sails across the boat for a change of direction, and we would have had to tack in this wind.

I didn't want to go into the cabin, so I moved to sit behind Jack. At least he couldn't say I was in his way. We were really moving now, but I felt the little craft was in good hands. Still, my heart was beating faster and I was more than pleased when we tied up at the Sound. The last manoeuvre would have been nearly impossible without the help of a man on the jetty. I had put out the fenders so that I didn't feel altogether useless.

"That was a bit of excitement," Jack said.

"Oom," I answered doubtfully, but I had felt the exhilaration of the danger and we ran, laughing, up to the village.

We hired a car to the hotel.

"If we're staying at the Emerald, you'd better book two rooms," I said.

"Why?" He looked shocked. "We could be miles apart."

"They know me there. We used to come here often for meals."

"But I want to sleep with you."

"I know."

"You think we should get married, don't you?"

"I do."

"Well, that's fine with me, you know that, as long as you don't mind being left, maybe for years at a time."

"I mind of course, but I love you and I want to marry you."

It was good to see this old hotel again.

"How are you?" the receptionist said. "We haven't seen you for ages. Where've you been?"

"I've been in London."

"You must be brave," she said.

"This is my fiancé, Jack Conway. He's the brave one. He's in the Navy."

"You're both very welcome," she said.

They were all good loyalists here and I was looking for their sympathy. She handed us a key each, 105 and 106.

"What did I tell you?" I said to Jack as we walked upstairs. There were no lifts here.

I loved this place. It still had the air of an aristocratic country house; the faded hand-painted wallpaper and the slightly worn Persian carpets. I searched the drawers in my room and was not surprised to find a key that fitted the adjoining door. It was a bit rusty, but it worked. Jack was surprised when I walked through.

"I've read about these country house-parties," I said.

"I could be ravished here," he said.

"Indeed you could," I said, "but not now. I'm starving and the food is scrumptious."

We went down to the dining room.

Chapter 19 – 1944

"Last time I was here I had lobster mayonnaise. It was delicious," I said to the waitress.

"Would you like that?"

"Yes please." Jack had the same, and while they were preparing the lunch, I rang John McBride. There were very few private telephones then. One small directory covered the whole country.

"Are any of my family around, John?" I said.

"Peter's here. I'll get him."

"Pete, will you tell them at home that we're at the Emerald and we won't leave till the wind dies down."

"Will do, hon." Peter was in the Air Corps.

I was dying to get out on the Atlantic Drive in the storm. We would have to drive to Dooega.

"You'll be blown away," the waitress said:

"It'll be a good excuse for hanging on to him, won't it?" I said.

I love these wild days in the west when nature calls the tune and we ignore her at our peril. This time she was doing us a real favour, giving us a night here.

We set out to walk to Ashleam. Surely we were on the wildest edge of the wild North Atlantic. Walking up the slope, it looked as if there were nowhere to go but over the cliff: then it swung sharply to the right. I had walked this way in the sunshine, but I had to see it doing its worst. I loved it, but I couldn't look over the edge the way Jack could.

"There's a wreck here," he said, when we got to Ashleam.

With the strange limestone stacks in the bay, Ashleam looked dramatic, and the wreck added to the drama.

"Of course, I'd forgotten. I was here when the court case was going on three years ago, but I left before it was over. I never heard the result."

"A merchant in Achill Sound ordered a cargo of coal. You might say gold, it's so scarce. That was in 1940 or '41. It was a Greek vessel and she went aground on the rocks here, but the merchant had her holds searched and there weren't two bags of coal in her. The Greek captain had sold the cargo, I don't know where, and then he ran her on to the rocks here, hoping to get away with it. She's a sad sight now."

There was a little café on the side of the bay and we decided to have a coffee while we got our breaths back.

"Oh, I haven't seen coffee since God knows when," the woman said. "There's that chicory, but you wouldn't count that. I have tea though. I get enough of that. I save it up in the winter. No one comes here then. Are ye English? I have nothing nice for ye only a few biscuits."

"No, we're not English, and tea will be lovely."

"Don't give her any biscuits, she's fat enough already," Jack said.

"Fat is it? God help us, if she turned sideways sure I wouldn't see her at all."

"Now if I'm going to marry her...."

Chapter 19 – 1944

"Sure she's too young to get married. Give her a chance."

"That's right," I said, "he's a cradle snatcher."

"Ye should have more sense than to be out on a day like this," she said.

"If we were English, we'd just be eccentric," I said when she'd gone. "You can get away with anything if you're English."

We left with her blessing. We decided to take the main road back to Dooega and I found myself wanting to cling tightly to Jack, not only because of the high wind. There's something erotic about islands. There was no one about. We were the only people left in the world and Jack wrapped his arms around me and gave me a long, long kiss.

"You taste salty," he said, and, laughing, we headed back into the spray. I wanted to get back to our room now, to have him to myself for a little while before dinner.

There were only two other couples staying in the hotel, one from Belfast and one from London. We all sat down to a memorable meal of Beef Wellington. The owner had dinner with us. She was a charming lady with a host of anecdotes to keep us laughing and to remind the rest of us of funny incidents in our own lives.

After dinner, the proprietor played the piano, and the Belfast couple, who had stayed here before and knew what to expect, brought down a mandolin and a guitar. It was a sentimental evening in that lovely room with a blazing fire, while the wind howled outside.

"Can we have one more night together," Jack said to me later. "We'll stay tomorrow night. O.K?" Then he said "If it's alright with you, we'll get married the next time I'm in Liverpool. That should be sometime in July. I'm afraid you'll have to make all the arrangements. It won't be easy."

This was a wonderful night for me, to be here in this lovely place with the man I loved and who would one day be the father of my children. The Emerald would always have a special place in my memory

Chapter 20

1944

It was wonderful to be together, and alone. "It will be a long time before we get a chance like this again," Jack said, and, with no regrets, our two days in Achill stretched to four.

On the Sunday morning we were ready to go home. Jack was looking forward to the trip on a lovely morning, but I liked to go to mass in the small country churches. In the Gaeltacht areas, people filled the churches and the forecourts in the summer and, although I could only get the gist of the sermons, I had a sense of being transported back in time.

I don't think Achill was Gaeltacht then. Most of the men and many of the girls migrated to Scotland on an annual basis for the potato harvest, so English was essential to them. I thought them a harder breed than the Gaeltacht people on the whole, having to cope with unbelievably harsh working and living conditions, and I wanted to join them in the one place that gave them self-respect. Jack was impatient to get going, but I was determined to go to church.

After the short delay, we were able to enjoy a perfect trip. It was warm for April and we skimmed along with a fair wind right in to our own pier. My father was there to make sure his pride and joy was properly moored. My mother was fond of saying that if her house was afloat he would be more eager about its maintenance. Jack seemed to see his point of view.

I had been in touch with the family about our extended stay and nothing was said about it now. Mother was fretting about Churchill's report in the Commons that fifty thousand civilians had been killed in air raids up to now.

"Why don't you stay here?" she said to me.

"I can't this time, Mum, we're getting married when Jack comes to Liverpool again."

"Getting married?" she sat down to get over the shock.

"Well, God direct you both." I went over and she hugged me. Then she kissed Jack. "When will it be?" she asked.

"Sometime in July. We'll try and have a date for the Registrar."

"We're hoping there'll be no problem," Jack said, "because there is a chance that the *Flint* will be among the ships going to France with the invasion fleet, whenever that will be."

My father came in and we told the story again. He shook hands with Jack. I knew he was pleased that I was marrying a sailor – someone he could talk to. He put his arm around me. "Look after her," he said.

We all had a drink then. The younger members of the family ran off to tell their friends and for a few hours, all was confusion. "What will you wear? Where will it be?" and, of course, "Will we be able to get there?"

I told them about Father O'Connor and St. Anselms and the Registrar and that I would be trying to get everything fixed up when we got back, but of course that everything depended on the invasion.

"No doubt they'll stop all travel in and out of the country so I wouldn't bank on being there if I were you. It will be the simplest affair, but maybe sometime in the future we'll have a big party with a wedding cake and everything – even a honeymoon – but now I'm going to find a pretty dress. If I can't get what I want in Westport, I'll have to search the theatrical shops in London. As usual I have no coupons left. He kind of sprung this on me."

I felt that I should be more excited, or sad or scared. I should be feeling more emotional, but everything was so uncertain. Even now it wouldn't surprise me if the whole thing had to be postponed. God knows what we were going back to. An invasion, U-boats, air raids. How could we be sure of anything.

Later we went into town to tell Jack's family. I was meeting them for the first time.

"You're welcome, you're very welcome," Jack's mother said, and we told her about the wedding.

"Well, thanks be to God," she said, "It takes marriage to make men of them."

I knew then that I would have a champion as long as she lived. Jack's father said little, but nodded his agreement. He was a handsome man, and dapper. He wore a cravat, which was out of the ordinary in Westport. He had a head wound from the First World War, when he had lost a leg as well. I wasn't sure how I felt about him. Formidable, was a word that came to mind.

"I saw you dancing on the stage a few years ago," my future mother-in-law said. "I was asking who you were then, and last year they told me that Jack was taking you out. He took long enough to ask you to marry him. The Lord keep you both safe to enjoy a long life together," she said. "You're living in dangerous times."

There were no hugs, no kisses, but I loved her.

Having spent so long in Achill, we still hadn't seen our friends Grace and Arthur. They had a hotel and a busy life, but they always had time for us.

"Where've you been?" Grace said when I rang. "We've been wondering when we were going to see you. Will you be in touch?"

"Yes, we'll see you tonight. I have something to tell you, but it can wait till then."

"I'll bet you two are engaged, aren't you?"

"If you mean that I have a diamond ring to show you, we're not and I haven't, but we do intend to get married when the *Flint Castle* is next in Liverpool."

Chapter 20 – 1944

"Well that's great news. I'm delighted for you both, and you can thank me, can't you? We'll have a party. When are you going back?"

"We'll be leaving on Wednesday."

"We'll have a party tomorrow night."

"Are you sure? It's such a lot of trouble."

"Of course I'm sure. We have to celebrate your engagement. Wasn't I in love with him long before you came along, but I'll forgive you. Come in tonight anyway and we'll have a quiet drink."

So we spent one of our last nights in Westport with our friends, as usual. In the small hours I went to my room and Jack came too, knowing that this would be our last night together before the momentous days ahead. I felt very emotional. How would the coming event affect us. How would I stand up to it all. Jack would take it in his stride, whatever happened, and maybe I wouldn't be too bad. I'd survived a lot already with more courage than I'd ever thought myself capable of. The last four years had made us all stronger.

Everyone knew that Hitler would make a last-ditch effort to salvage what was left of the Third Reich. The war which had started with Germany's high hopes was not going to be allowed to become Germany's despair if he could help it. We had heard of his deadly secret weapons and that hazard was still ahead of us.

I had the feeling of standing on the edge of a precipice which we were both going to have to face alone, before we met briefly to make the promises which would blind us for the rest of our lives, even though we might be hundreds or thousands of miles apart.

"It's not going to be easy for two normally passionate young people to keep the rules," Jack said.

"I want to have a baby as soon as I can," I said. "That will keep me busy."

"And I'll have you to come back to," he said. "We'll be alright."

Two days later, in Liverpool, I telephoned Father O'Connor and made an appointment to see him. I told him that Jack expected to be back in Liverpool sometime in July and we wanted to be married.

"I'll be here to marry you, Frances," he said. "You'd better get in touch with the Registrar. Have you got the address I gave you?"

"It's among my things in London," I said, "but I won't know the exact date until they're home again. Twenty-four hours' notice is the most we'll have, and even less time together after we're married – a lot less, I expect."

"You'll need a lot of love and trust, Frances," he said.

"I have no doubts, Father," I said.

I arrived back in London to quiet night's half-way through April. I was busy at work, but spent my spare time trawling the theatrical shops for the sort of dress I wanted and, before long, I found it in Shaftesbury Avenue. It was a pink silk 'twenty-ish' looking outfit, and it was minute.

Chapter 20 – 1944

"That would have looked good on Anna Neagle in her younger days," the girl said, "and that's who I thought of when you came in."

She wrapped it carefully in tissue for travelling, but I knew I would have to show it to the girls, and July was months away.

Now Eleanor was pressing to me 'marry' her. "Peter needs you and I need you." In her opinion, girls who would rescue a toddler from a freezing bath and wrap him in a blanket were few and far between, and shouldn't waste their energy on anything other than child-minding, and Eleanor-minding, of course.

I laughed. Treating the whole thing as a joke would be the best way to handle it, I thought.

"I'm going to marry Jack Conway in July," I said.
"Oh, bloody men," she said. She and Alan had married before the war and Peter was their second child. The first was being cared for by Eleanor's old nanny in the country and, up to now, Peter had lived in a residential nursery while his mother studied medicine. She and Alan had fallen out of love years ago, she said, and they only got together when she wanted another child.

"I want all my children to have the same father," she told me as though she personally had invented a new mode of living. Now she hoped to install a surrogate mother for Peter in the new flat while she pursued her career in the Chelsea Hospital for Women.

American bombers were attacking military installations now, not only on the Normandy coast but in the Pas de Calais, so we knew that the big day couldn't be far off, although it was still impossible to guess where the troops might land. We only felt that it would be pretty soon.

In the meantime, life and work were proceeding normally. There was no outward sign of panic anywhere. As far as we young people were concerned, there was little to be lost. Like the snail, we carried pretty well all we owned on our backs. So for the moment all was quiet. The calm before the storm, no doubt.

In Italy there was a different story. Half-way through May a major offensive began under General Alexander, backed by the United States Air Corps. The Germans were outnumbered several times, but it was a bitter fight. Someone had said that if you fought the Germans, you knew you'd been in a war, or words to that effect. It was obvious what they meant, judging by the newspapers.

Everything now pointed to the imminence of the Invasion. The U.S. Air Corps was systematically destroying the railways in Northern France. There was activity in the Dover region, as well as further west, but the north-eastern counties were also active, pointing to a possible invasion of Norway. They would keep the Germans guessing.

Chapter 20 – 1944

The training programme for the invasion forces was tough, no doubt. At the Overseas Club we would meet the Americans who had been on British rations during training and they wondered how we hadn't all starved to death.

After training, there was a week's leave and they thronged London that week. Quaglino's, the Hungaria, the Overseas Club, Rainbow Corner, every place was filled with pleasure-seeking men – and women.

'We who are about to die…'

We danced and laughed with them and, somehow, managed to go home alone. It took a lot of good humour and sympathy because, for many, it would be their last week in this world.

I wrote a poem for those who would not come back:

Do you remember the night we met
By the railings on Hammersmith Broadway
I calling 'taxi'
While you called 'cab'
But nobody stopped
And we looked at each other
And laughed
On Hammersmith Broadway.

I taught you the words of 'Galway Bay'
While we waited on Hammersmith Broadway
Londoners listened

And everyone laughed
At the star-spangled rhythm
Of chorus and verse
That rang out
Over Hammersmith Broadway.

I'll see you home,
We'll meet again,
I'll call you every evening
And so it was for ten short days
Till the D-Day force was leaving.

Now we won't meet again
And we won't sing again
Alas
On Hammersmith Broadway.

As we guessed earlier, all travel in and out of the country was stopped. The south coast was out of bounds also. There would be no more holidays this year. Suddenly, home was a long way away, Jack was out of reach and our future was in the hands of the gods.

In Italy, the troops had at last broken out of the Anzio beachhead and linked up with those coming from the south. Then, on the evening of the 4th June, the Americans marched into Rome, but news of the capture of the first European capital was overshadowed by the coming invasion.

The Allies had suffered forty thousand casualties in the drive for Rome. The city was dearly bought. As one soldier said, "Only the suffering was real."

The Irish Guards had been in the thick of the fighting from the start, and when they pulled out of the beachhead on the 7th March, two hundred and sixty-seven men survived of the thousand and more who had landed.

Monsignor O'Flaherty requested the Pope to receive the regiment in audience before they left Rome, and one of the guardsmen, overcome with emotion, gave the Pope his blessing.

"I hope God will bless me, my son," the Pope said.

A Nightingale Sang

Chapter 21

1944

The bad weather at the beginning of June delayed the invasion by twenty-four hours, but on the evening of the 5th, the Supreme Commander, General Eisenhower, gave the order for the launch of the greatest seaborne invasion in history. The weather was still abominable, but further delay would have meant postponing the whole massive operation for a month.

The Germans considered that a fine spell of four consecutive days would be essential. Therefore, from the Allied point of view, a landing in bad weather would be to their advantage.

Dummy runs were set up in the Boulogne and Calais areas on the 5th June to confuse the waiting Germans, but on the morning of the 6th, we knew that D-day had arrived. Five hundred thousand men, in thousands of Allied ships under the command of the Royal Navy, had been landed on the Normandy beaches. Half a million men, many of them still in their teens, frightened and seasick, were back on the Continent.

Half a million men landed on the 6th June 1944, but before the day was over, ten thousand were killed or wounded. The Americans landing on the beach they called Omaha, met the full force of the German defence.

Four long war-torn years had passed since the evacuation of the British Expeditionary Force from Dunkirk, and now they were going back, to God knows what.

By dawn on the 6th, eighteen thousand paratroops had also been dropped. At 6.30am the first American soldiers landed at Utah Beach. The oldest among them was General Teddy Roosevelt, F.D.R's son, and he proudly pointed out his own son, Quentin, to the soldiers. He died of a heart attack in Normandy a month later.

The Canadians arrived at Juno and the British at Gold and Sword.

We got some first-hand information about the landings much sooner than we expected because one of the boys we knew arrived home with a broken leg. He had been dropped with the American parachutists, but had broken his leg in the fall. He felt that the whole scene would be sketched clearly on his mind for the rest of his life.

The Canadians, who had learned from bitter experience two years earlier at Dieppe, did get all their brigades ashore on D-day, although they suffered a thousand casualties on Juno Beach. They continued to press inland, however, and before nightfall had secured their bridgehead.

Chapter 21 – 1944

Cynthia and I watched these incredible scenes later on the cinema newsreels. We could only imagine the feelings of the men approaching the windswept cost of France that dawn, frightened and seasick as they were. It was described as the greatest mass-seasickness ever, and it accelerated a cure for that unpleasant complaint.

The houses along the seafront were forlorn shells from the preceding naval bombardment. Where were their owners, we wondered, and what were their feelings about the invasion?

People on the south coast of England, and particularly the major port of Southampton, saw the departure of the immense armada, heard the cheers from the other ships in the harbour and, occasionally, the incomparably moving caoin of the bagpipes. It was an emotional time.

Of all the men who embarked for France on the 5th/6th June 1944, ten thousand were killed, wounded or missing; on Omaha Beach alone there were about two thousand casualties on the first day.

A week after D-day, the night of the 13th/14th June, I woke up to see a plane flying low past my window. The room was a blaze of light and I rushed to the window expecting to see a plane in trouble. The engine sounded rougher than usual. I could see the flame coming from the tail plane. It looked like a plane on fire, and it was hardly out of sight when there was a massive explosion. Then everything was quiet again and I went back to sleep.

In the morning it was reported that a German plane had crashed on a gas holder in Bethnal Green. That was all the Germans wanted to know, that the first of Hitler's deadly secret weapons had reached its target, London. This would become known as the V-1, or flying bomb, which looked like a small plane and carried a ton of high explosive in its warhead.

It was the start of a murderous campaign which killed more people in London than had died on the Normandy beaches. Night and day they came over without respite. At work we were reassured about the position of the building and the fact that there were adequate shelters.

In the first three days, two hundred and fifty people were killed; over a hundred in the Guards Chapel at Wellington Barracks on the Sunday. It was a favourite place of worship for Londoners during the way years.

The RAF and the U.S. Air Force intensified their bombing campaign on the flying bomb sites on the continent, and we knew that many of the flying bombs crossing the coast were shot down before they reached the London area. The Government worried about the effect this second bombing campaign would have on a people already becoming war-weary, and every deterrent was being mounted to counteract it.

Chapter 21 – 1944

By the third week in June there were half a million Allied soldiers in France and some of them would have orders to capture and destroy the flying bomb launching sites.

Travelling to work one morning on the top of the bus, it was strange to watch all the windows in the shops along the Kings Road imploding while we, surrounded by glass, were unaffected. We had not heard the explosion and there was no noise of crashing glass. It was like watching a silent film.

That lunch hour, Lyn was in the Strand, with thousands of other people, when a flying bomb hit the top of Somerset House and exploded prematurely. Above the noise of the traffic, Lyn heard the engine cut out and, anticipating the explosion, she warned two men who were passing. Then she lay down on the pavement and covered her head with her briefcase. When the bomb exploded, she was hurt with falling masonry, but had probably saved her life with the briefcase. It had taken some courage to lie down on the busy street.

Rumours spread like wildlife from every bombing incident and we, although a couple of miles away, heard that the V-1 had come down on Somerset House. It caused panic in our group because the husband of one of the girls worked there.

"I must get down there," she said. Her face was ashen and she looked as though she would faint. "I wonder if I can get a taxi."

"I doubt it," somebody said. "I'm pretty sure they'll be wanted at the bombsite. Maybe you could get a bus. It would take you most of the way. It won't get into the Strand."

"I'll come with you," her friend said. She certainly needed someone. We all hoped and prayed that she would find her husband alive and this, happily, turned out to be the case.

Because the V-1's were more likely to explode at any time of the day in Central London, a new warning was introduced. Klaxens were sounded to indicate immediate danger, but that day in the Strand, the explosion was caused by the impact with Somerset House was unexpected and there were no klaxens. The tragic result was that two hundred people were killed, and they probably included the two men who had assured Lyn that there was no immediate danger.

Lyn spent the following few days in hospital. She was badly frightened. I went to see her. She was not too badly hurt, mainly cuts and grazing on her back and legs.

"I'm not staying in London any longer," she said. "It's crazy to put up with all this when we could be in Bournemouth or somewhere." I didn't like the way she said "we".

"Will you come with me if we can find jobs?"

"I honestly don't want to leave London," I said. "I don't find the flying bombs any more frightening than the ordinary air raids. Rather less so, in fact. At least there's no man up there making a deliberate decision to kill or maim whoever happens to be underneath."

Chapter 21 – 1944

"What difference does that make? You can get killed just the same. Besides, there's worse to come. What about these V-2s they're talking about?"

The V-2s were the rocket bombs we had been warned about. They were said to be far more dangerous. They would travel faster than sound, would reach London in three or four minutes and would explode without warning. They would carry ten tons of high explosive.

It sounded terrifying and I said I would be prepared to leave if they were as bad as they said.

I had just returned from the hospital and was going upstairs when the telephone rang.

"Oh, you're there."

It was two years since I'd heard his voice and I was surprised.

"Tom?"

"Last time I rang you were in Ireland. I was afraid you wouldn't come back. Whoever answered the phone didn't have an address to give me, but he told me that someone else had your room."

"Oh, that was ages ago. I didn't stay very long, but you had left England when I came back. Are you on leave?"

"No, they've brought us back to deal with the flying bombs. We're already having some success. Yesterday was the best day so far. We shot down several. Barely half of them got through to London and we seem to be bagging more of them every day."

"We have a lot to be grateful to you for. It's been very bad, thousands killed and so much damage done."

"As long as you're alright. When can I see you? I'm off tomorrow night."

"Do you want to go to a concert or anything?"

"No, I want to talk to you. Can we go to that pub?"

"The Six Bells? Where we went before? I could meet you at eight if that's alright." It was only five minutes' walk away.

So, the following evening I met Tom Faulkener for the first time in two years. It was good to see him again. I had felt sad and guilty about our last conversation on the telephone when I'd dismissed his marriage proposal because 'I was busy'. It had been a particularly frantic afternoon, but that was no excuse.

I had known Tom since schooldays, but now I sensed a big change. He had been through life-threatening times, in the thick of the trouble since the fall of Greece. I had never understood why he joined the Marines, the toughest of men, this sensitive boy I knew at college, but he had learnt to hold his own and, apparently, had some good friends.

We had several drinks before the sirens went. There wasn't a lot to recommend the drinks. They came already mixed in the bottle, moonshine you might call it, with an orange coloured mix. We were becoming immune to the poison. It loosened the tongue and we spent hours recalling the good times. Then Tom was holding my hands and telling me that he loved me.

"May I come home with you?" he said.

"Tom," I said, "I'm getting married."

He looked crestfallen. "I should have known, but let me come back with you this once. We've known each other for a very long time, haven't we?"

I had to put an end to this conversation.

"I'd better be getting home," I said. "These bombs are coming closer."

"I'll walk down with you," he said.

We were already outside the house, but I knew that I shouldn't ask him in, although it wasn't easy to turn my old friend away. All those nights when we'd caught the last train home after Sadlers Wells or Covent Garden had all ended with a friendly kiss. I didn't think either of us had expected anything more. But had I chosen to ignore the fact that Tom had always been in love with me? Anyway, it was obviously different now and I didn't want to play with fire.

"I'm sure you don't want dandelion coffee," I said, and we giggled about that.

"I don't want coffee, Fran, I want you."

"Tom, I'm getting married next month."

"Why aren't you marrying me? You turned me down and he won't be half as nice to you as I would be."

"No one is half as nice as you Tom, but nature doesn't care a damn about that. Nature is a trumpet. No, that's not the word. Nature is a strumpet, that's it. Didn't someone say that? They should have. Nature is a trollop. This can't go any further

Tom. It wouldn't help anyone in the long run. We have to say goodbye now."

"I've wanted you for years, Fran. I wish I'd had the courage to tell you so two years ago. Things might have turned out differently. Let me come in with you. You can't leave me out here to the mercy of these bombs."

"Oh, come in. I'll make tea."

It was fatal. Inside the door he put his arms around me. "You can't send me home tonight."

It took a long time to persuade him to sleep in the spare bed. I didn't sleep. It was relief of a kind to share my night with the flying bombs that were exploding intermittently at some distance. I had closed the shutters as a precaution, so the noise of their flight was muffled to some extent and I couldn't see the fire that belched from their tails.

I got up early and made tea. I poured a cup for Tom and left it on the small chest beside the divan. He woke up with the next explosion.

"How can you stand those bloody bombs?" he said, which made me laugh considering what his company was going through on the Downs.

"Oh, it is not half as bad when you can hit back," he said. "Come here, you're miles away."

Chapter 21 – 1944

I sat on the bed.

"Thank you for letting me stay. I hope I wasn't too much of a nuisance," he said. "I'll always remember how sweet you are. I'll always have that."

I felt a constriction in my throat. I knew I would never see my old friend again.

A Nightingale Sang

Chapter 22

1944

The flying bomb menace continued through June and into July. We knew that the Marines were doing their best to prevent them getting through to London. They had one battery on the coast and another on the North Downs and more V-1's were being shot down every day.

I was preparing for my wedding. This meant collecting my prettiest underwear, a couple of pairs of shoes and something to travel in. I put them all into a suitcase with the precious pink outfit. I would have no more than a few hours warning. Jack would telephone when they got in, I would catch the next train and we would be married the following day. Within twenty-four hours I'd be back in London and he would be on the high seas. What times we live in.

Getting married during the war didn't entail looking for a house or buying furniture, although the furniture available was of good quality, even if the design was basic. Early in the war, the Government introduced standards in furniture and clothing which had to be adhered to and all bore a CC41 logo. They were known as Utility, and the furniture would, no doubt, outlive its owners. It would have been an excellent time to buy a house, had one been a gambler, but the thought of owning anything other than, maybe, a radio, never entered our heads. We were footloose and there was no feeling then of ever being anything else. "When the war is over" usually meant no more than having the men back, and to me it didn't even mean that. Jack was in the Navy for the foreseeable future and only the thought of having a family kept me from adopting the same nomadic existence.

A suitcase full of fripperies was all I needed.

We were all upset to hear that most of the people who were killed when a flying bomb hit St Mary Abbot's Hospital in Kensington were children, and then, at the end of June, there was a second incident involving children when a V-1 falling outside London killed several infants under twelve months who had been evacuated for safety. One of them was a month old.

About two thousand people had been killed in the two weeks since the V-1s were launched.

During the first week in July when a flying bomb fell in Lambeth, American servicemen were transported across the river to help with the wounded. About seventy more men were waiting on the pavement outside their depot near Sloane Square for trucks to take them across, when another flying bomb exploded in Chelsea, killing most of the men and several civilians in the vicinity. That one was close enough to knock me over as I was dressing for work.

Chapter 22 – 1944

So many people had been killed in London by the end of that week, that the Prime Minister ordered the release of the new drug, Penicillin, for the treatment of civilians. So far it had been used only for the forces.

On the continent, where the army needed a port, it was a relief to know that Cherbourg had fallen and the fight for Caen was on.

At home, I was getting nervous. Was it the flying bombs? Was it the telephone call that would change my life, or was I afraid that Jack's ship would not be coming back and there would be no telephone call? It must be soon, I thought. It was. Early in the morning on the 8th July, the telephone rang.

"Hello honey. Are you ready for the big day? There's a train at three."

I was delighted to hear him. My fears dissolved. "I am now. You're welcome back. I'll see you soon."

I took a taxi from Lime Street Station to the Royal George that evening and Jack joined me there. We told our friend the receptionist that we were taking her advice and she promised to drink a toast with us.

Jack should have been on watch that evening, but someone took pity on him so that we could have a few more hours together. He would be back on the ship at 8 a.m.

After breakfast I tried to ring Father O'Connor, but he was not at the presbytery. I explained the situation. He had promised to marry us when Jack returned to Liverpool, that the ship would be sailing first thing in the morning, so it would have to be today. They promised to try and find the priest. After a nerve-racking series of telephone calls, which included the unhelpful Registrar, it was established that three o'clock would be the time for the wedding and St. Anselm's Church the place.

I had a typical wartime lunch and returned to the hotel to find that Jack was already there. He scooped me up in his arms and danced across the foyer.

"Come on, we'll have a drink," he said. He had spent the morning celebrating in the wardroom.

"I have to get dressed," I said.

"But you look great..."

"You wait in the bar. I'll be as quick as I can. We have to be at St. Anselm's at three."

"You look lovely," he said when I came back." The receptionist'll have to see you."

We took a taxi to the sad grey church standing alone in the docklands. I would never forget the eerie silence as I stood there clinging to Jack's hand. There was a feeling of being the only people left in a world destroyed by war. It would be up to us to start a whole new world.

At ten to three the registrar arrived and took a seat without looking to either left or right, and, to my relief, Fr.

Chapter 22 – 1944

O'Connor arrived five minutes later. His hands were full, but he stretched a couple of free fingers in my direction. "I wouldn't let you down, Frances," he said. He introduced the girl he had promised to bring as my bridesmaid. Jack's friend, the best man, stepped out from behind him. He looked nervous and had waylaid the priest to enquire about his 'duties'. He kissed me and said that the others would meet us at the hotel. I handed him the wedding ring I had bought in London.

I was in a dream world now, barely conscious of the ceremony which would bind us 'from this day forward as long as we both should live.'

There were kisses all round and then we were in the taxi returning to the George.

Jack put his arms around me. "Hardly an ideal wedding I suppose, but we'll be alright. There's nothing I wouldn't do for you now."

When we got back to the hotel, with so little time left to sailing, there was a tacit decision to by-pass the proposed party.

Jack opened a bottle of champagne in our room, but I drank very little, determined that nothing should blunt the memories of this night, even to the last sad goodbye before the dawn. These were the memories which would enhance the good times ahead and help me over the bad. I would be in love with this man for the rest of my life.

Tomorrow the *Flint Castle* would sail down the Mersey into the Atlantic to pick up the next convoy off Moville or Greenock. She would weave in and out among her charges scattered over a whole expanse of the ocean. Night and day, in fine weather or storms, thirty or forty ships would be watched and guarded, any messages delivered painfully from the barrel of a gun. They were our lifeline and we could only pray for their safety.

I would return to London and the flying bombs.

It was still dark when Jack tiptoed out of our room like an illicit lover; out into the silence of blacked-out Liverpool, and I was left to cry alone. I looked at my watch. It was five-fifteen and the hotel was deadly silent. I hadn't a hope of going back to sleep again and breakfast wouldn't be served for hours. I decided to get dressed and go downstairs. If the night porter was around he might make me a cup of coffee. He might even be in the mood for a chat. Anything was better than lying here alone.

By seven o'clock, after three coffees, I was on first-name terms with the porter's entire family.

There was porridge for my wedding breakfast, but the waitress felt sorry for me and she did all she could. She gave me a small pot of golden syrup to sweeten the porridge. I made a dash for the station.

Chapter 22 – 1944

The stores which Jack had managed to acquire – eggs packed to survive a ship rolling, dried fruit and brown sugar, had made my case too heavy to carry. A young porter came to my aid. He stayed with me in the long queue during the interminable wait for the train. I would always remember that, and the way he called me 'ma'am when he saw the wedding ring, although I was about his own age. Would anyone else ever call me ma'am I wondered.

I stood with you yesterday
in a sad grey church
on a bombed out street
in a city where nobody knew me

I held your hand
fearful for you.
Sleep with me tonight, you said,
tomorrow I'll sail down the Mersey

We'll pick up a convoy off Moville
of British tramps and trawlers
We'll keep them together
or tell them to scatter
to dodge the hidden wolf-packs.

So today I'm alone on the London train
looking at my brand-new wartime wedding ring
thinking of my brand-new brave husband
dodging U-boats.

My first attempt to make a fruit cake was a heroic failure, but I invited the others to share the soufflé I made with the eggs and we all enjoyed a rare feast.

Although I had been reluctant to give Lyn a promise to leave London, we heard that people were evacuating the city in even larger numbers than had left during the Blitz. Maybe I would change my mind if the rockets came.

My life had changed without any regrets. At the Overseas Club they were dancing to 'Kalamazoo' and 'The American Patrol' Well, I did miss dancing I suppose, but I was going to spend my evenings at home.

I'll walk alone
Although to tell you the truth I am lonely…

I could still sing, and I did, loudly, one evening when there was no one else in the house, but to my horror a little nose appeared out of a hole which should have taken a gas pipe down to the nether regions. I quickly put a flower pot over the hole. Did the mice have a secret life under the floorboards, I wondered. I could have set a trap, but the thought of seeing one dead was even less attractive than having beady eyes staring at me any time I happened to break into song. The flower pot became a permanent fixture.

During August, no more than forty flying bombs reached the London area, but hundreds of people were killed. By the end of the month, the Marines on the Downs were becoming deadly accurate. The day came when, of the hundred or so V-1s which crossed the coast, only three got through to London. Those not shot down by anti-aircraft fire were destroyed by the RAF. We were grateful to the men who were making Trojan efforts to save us from this life-threatening menace.

A Nightingale Sang

Chapter 23

1944

Of all the nostalgic songs written and sung through the war years, one of the most popular was 'The Last Time I saw Paris'. People remembered the city with affection and were sad that it was far out of reach to us all those years. It was great now to hear that the Allies were on their way back.

When that news appeared in the press, I was reminded of my last visit during the Easter holidays before the war when I danced in the Tuileries Gardens with a Hungarian friend, very early one morning. It was such sheer joy to be in that lovely city on a beautiful morning. My friend lived in Paris. I wonder where he is now.

The first news was that General Patton had broken out of Normandy and was a hundred and sixty kilometres from Paris. Then, half-way through August the Allies landed at St. Tropez on the south coast of France, but they were not moving fast enough for the French partisans. Paris started its own upraising. The Resistance, the police and a rare Parisian mixture of Communists, Anarchists, Gaullists and Monarchists called the city to battle with 'Tous aux Barricades'. Every day rumours reached London while we watched the advance of the Allied armies.

By the 23rd August, the Americans had made Paris their objective. On the 24th, every church bell in the city was ringing and the great French national anthem was played constantly.

Early on the 25th, the Sherman tanks began to roll in and the entire population came out to greet them. The city went wild. So many girls climbed onto the tanks that the order "Allons les femmes – Descendez ..." had to be given before attacks on the German strong points could begin.

Simone de Beauvoir wrote that to be twenty in 1944 was a rare stroke of good luck.

It was said that few soldiers slept alone the night Paris was liberated. One officer, returning late to his battalion, said he preferred to draw a veil over what he found there.

General Leclerc, with his French division, was the first to enter Paris and at 2.30 on the afternoon of the 25th August, the German Commander surrendered to him. Not long afterwards de Gaulle arrived. The following day his giant figure was seen on the newsreels of the world leading a triumphal march down the Champs Elysees. It was the fulfilment of his four-year-old dream.

When Montgomery discovered how eager his soldiers were to get to the red light districts, he sent in the military police. That was when the fields around the camps were pressed into service in pursuit of l'amour. How to get them back to the farm now?

De Gaulle had little regard for the Resistance whose views were in stark contrast to his own. He set up a Provisional Government, emphasising that everything should be as it was before he left.

The punishments for collaboration with the enemy were severe by any standards, particularly in cases of 'collaboration horizontale'. There was no Gallic mercy for women who had slept with the Germans. Most of the Allied soldiers were shocked and sickened by these punishments.

In London, on the 7th September, the Government announced that the menace of the V-1s was over, but no sooner had the announcement been made than the first V-2 exploded. This time the Germans would not be told that the rocket bomb had reached its target. That news was first reported in the New York Times and, by the middle of September, there were regular explosions and hundreds of people had been killed.

I knew now that Lyn would be expecting me to make a decision about leaving, especially after the explosion in South London which killed a hundred and sixty people one lunch hour. Horrific stories were beginning to circulate from the bomb sites and I felt sure she would think it crazy to remain in the city if we didn't have to.

Up to now I had found the rockets no more terrifying than anything that had happened previously. There were no sirens and no agonising anticipation. There was a deafening explosion and then it was all over until the next time and, of course, there was always the human feeling that it would never happen to you.

I hated the thought of leaving London and starting again in a strange place. I enjoyed being part of the social revolution which the war was bringing about and I felt that the provinces would be removed from the excitement. Lyn was still sleeping at the Air Ministry, so the best thing would be to meet her for lunch. I rang.

"How are you?" I enquired. "I haven't seen you for ages. I was wondering if we could meet for lunch. I'll come over to the Aldwych."

"Are you coming to Bournemouth with me?" she said.

There was no avoiding it. "I was hoping you weren't going to ask. I'm not that scared yet, but we'll talk about it." I knew nothing would persuade me to go. Lyn was very disappointed with me.

We talked about the war instead, where the Allies were doing well on the continent. The British advance had been so fast that already their supply lines were overstretched. They had Antwerp but it was unusable because the Germans occupied an island at the entrance to the port.

Because the Allies had not yet been able to break through the German defences on the Dutch border. Montgomery conceived a plan to drop the first Parachute

Regiment behind the lines. The area around Arnhem on the Rhine was chosen. Montgomery gambled on their taking the main bridges on the Rhine, joining up with the ground forces advancing into Germany, and ending the war before Christmas.

Already the British supply lines were over four hundred and fifty miles long and General Patton had advanced four hundred miles from his source of supplies, so there were genuine fears from the start that Arnhem was 'a bridge too far', but Montgomery was willing to take the risk.

It was a combined operation of British, American and Polish troops, but the German defences in the area were much stronger than had been anticipated and the fighting was bitter and costly, with incredible stories of courage among the men involved. After nine days the survivors surrendered. Thousands of men died or were captured at Arnhem and five Victoria Crosses were awarded FOR VALOUR. Four of the awards were posthumous.

Arnhem was captured by the Canadians only weeks before VE-Day.

On the 2nd September, there was no mistaking the Irish Guards regiment which arrived in Brussels. Their tanks were dedicated to St. Patrick, Connaught, Leinster, Achill, Ulster and Bantry – all named by men who were nostalgic for home after five years of war. They were given a rousing welcome, but, following an advance of a hundred and eighty miles without sleep, they were too exhausted even to return the girls' embraces. They left the next morning for Nijmegan where, after a decisive defeat of the Germans, they were sent to the rear for a rest.

It was said of the Irish Guards that they did only what the other guards did, but they did it with more flair. Reading their latest achievements took me back to the night before the war when I had travelled from Dublin with them. I wondered how many of them had survived. That night they had been so eager for war. By now they'd surely had enough of it.

Now the Germans were shelling Folkestone and Dover from across the Channel and, as the V-2s continued their destruction of London, plans were being laid for the evacuation of the city.

Chapter 24

1944

When the ban on travel out of the country was lifted, I still had some leave to come, so I decided to go home. It had been a wearisome time since the night I watched the first V-1 flying past my window, and when I heard that a girl from my old school had arranged to study medicine in Trinity College, Dublin, I made up my mind to travel to Ireland with her. I was looking forward to meeting Joan again.

"Why Dublin?," I said to her when we met at Euston.

"In a way it's a surprise to me too," she said. "I met an Irishman a year ago who is already at Trinity. We wanted to meet again so I applied to the college and was accepted. I've always wanted to do medicine, as I think you know, but I thought I'd wait until after the war. However, when I met Harry, the thought of getting away from the bombs appealed to me. So did the opportunity of being with him. I'm really looking forward to it."

"Didn't I hear that you were working on the Grand Union Canal?"

"Yes, I thought it would be fun to try that for a while. I've been transporting cargo on a barge from London to Birmingham. We were given six days to do the journey."

"It's certainly different."

"Yes, I've enjoyed it I suppose, although it was often cold and messy. The old canal hasn't been properly cleaned since the war started, so the propeller blades were likely to get fouled up with weeds. That meant getting down there and clearing them, which could be tedious if it happened too often."

"Was it boring? Six days seems a long time for that trip."

"No, I've been writing about my experiences with a Jewish family in Munchen-Gladbach in Germany before the war, and I could write in my spare time. I doubt if I would have been able to do that if I'd stayed in London."

"Oh yes. What happened to that family? Have you ever heard?"

"Well the SS came for Heiner one night and took him away. That was before I left. Apparently he was made to lie on the luggage rack on the train and the guards kept poking them to keep them awake and to keep them facing the light. It was torture. Renate managed to get to America with the children. I haven't heard from her for some time now, but I'm, hoping to contact her again to get the end of the story.

"How long are you staying in Ireland?" she asked.

"Oh, I'll be back within the week. We haven't been allowed to leave the country since before the invasion. I expect that's why there are so many people going home now. I'll be glad of the rest. London's had more than its share of drama since June."

"I don't know how you could live there all the time. A few days every fortnight was more than enough for me."

Chapter 24 – 1944

"I have a feeling it's more frightening in small doses. One can get used to anything, even sleepless nights and bombing."

"You're welcome to it," she said. "You've always had this feeling for London, haven't you? Where's your friend Margaret now?"

"She joined the WAAF. She married a squadron leader, but he was shot down in a raid on Berlin. She was pregnant at the time. The baby is a month old now."

"That's awful. I'm so sorry. Your husband is in the Navy, isn't he?"

"Yes, he's on Atlantic convoys. I'm just hoping he won't be sent to the Far East. As it is I can see him fairly often.

"Here we are at Chester already. Do you want a mug of their awful tea?"

The time passed quickly while we caught up on all the news. We managed to get a cabin on the ship and slept for a good three hours. I had seldom found the journey less tedious. I left Joan with her friend in Dun Laoghaire and took the train to Westland Row, and on to the West.

It was good to be home again. I was hardly inside the door when two of my sisters were making plans for me to go to a dance with them that night. They were all growing up while my back was turned.

"I haven't been to a dance since I got married," I said.

"Two whole months," they hooted. "You can't stop dancing just because you're married."

"Well, it's different in Westport I suppose. Everybody knows me. In London it's too much trouble. All those lonely men."

"Sounds great," Florence said. She had turned into quite a beauty with her off-the-shoulder broderie Anglaise blouse showing off her summer tan. She was as dark as I was fair, a younger edition of our mother. Were we still allowed to call her Lollipop, I wondered.

"I'm not complaining," I said.

"O.K. we'll all go to the dance and we'll all come home together. How's that?"

"Oh, don't let me spoil your chances. I'm sure I can stay with Grace."

I'd had a lot of fun dancing in Westport whenever I was on leave. I knew all the good dancers and they didn't desert me now.

> '*Casey was there with a strawberry blonde*
> *And the band played on ...*'

The last dance I was at here, Jack and I had walked around the lake in the demesne getting to know each other. Now I missed him so much, it was painful.

> '*He married the girl with the strawberry curl*
> *And the band played on.*'

I don't think I'll ever want to dance without him again.

Chapter 24 – 1944

The girls arranged a party and Grace arranged a party, I visited my in-laws and I relished the peace and fun of the place I loved. Flying bombs and rockets had no place here. They were like a bad dream.

"Who's going to climb the Reek with me tomorrow?" I never left Westport without climbing Croagh Patrick.

"We'll all go. Are we going to walk?"

"We always do, don't we?" I said.

"We thought you might have gone weak on those rations over there."

"We'll walk out anyway, and I reckon after eating in Campbells we'll be fit for the walk back."

"Campbells?" they all shrieked.

"I'm telling you, bacon and eggs, sausages and wild mushrooms and Mrs. Campbell's brown bread, and we'll be fit for anything." I'd had experience of Mrs. Campbell's food.

It was a five-mile walk to the foot of the mountain, then a two and a half thousand feet climb and the long walk home. On the pilgrimage Sunday at the end of July we used to be ready for the dance in the evening. There were no softies in our house.

"Rory O'Brien came with us last time. Is he at home?" I asked.

They all looked at me. "Didn't I tell you?" my mother said. "Rory was killed in the war".

"On no! I thought he was studying medicine in Dublin."

"Oh, the forces were more exciting," she said sadly.

"What a terrible loss. All those young men with their lives ahead of them. I'll have to see Mrs. O'Brien," I said.

"They'll never get over it," my mother said.

Thinking of Rory's death certainly took the joy out of our plans for the next day. I couldn't help thinking how my circle of friends and relatives had been reduced by this dreadful war. I thought, not only of those who had been killed, but of the very special people like Sandy and Tom who were out of my life forever. I would probably never even talk about them again.

"Alright, will we be ready to leave at eight o'clock in the morning?" I said. This was not a pilgrimage, but there is something very special about that mountain. Like Skellig or Clonmacnoise, there are no words for it.

We would take water bottles with us and fill them from the crystal-clear stream running down the mountain.

We woke up to what is euphemistically known as 'local drizzle' and told ourselves that this would make the climb easier because the stones would be embedded in the softer earth instead of sliding under our feet. We knew all that mountain's peculiarities.

It was an enjoyable day. The mist cleared before we got to the summit and we had a splendid view of the bay to the north and the boglands that skirted Croagh Patrick to the south and, beyond them, the ancient mountains of Connemara. My mind expanded to take it all in. Why didn't I stay here where life had a third dimension. Why did I chose that well-ordered existence where time is tethered to mans' needs when God has given us this beautiful land to grow in? Still. I knew I would go back. I knew that, because this time there was the very real hope of seeing Jack again soon. This would make up for everything.

I left on the early train. Travel had improved quite a bit in the country. There was more coal available for the railways, so the journey to Dublin was faster now than it had been early in the war.

The small country stations were crowded, as usual these days. The men had to go where the work was, in the war-torn cities of the neighbouring island, often leaving wives and children at home. It had happened so often in our history, it was hardly surprising that Irishmen were strangers to their families. Would there be a generation in time to come that would call a halt to this ruination of family life?

On the boat an old man handed me his embarkation card to fill in. "I haven't me glasses with me" was his excuse. He was of an age when he should have been able to enjoy evenings by the fire at home, but the money to be earned in England was a scarce commodity in the villages of the west. Cromwell didn't mean to do us any favours when he drove us west of the Shannon.

At Euston, the hard tones of the Londoners would jar on the ear until I became accustomed to them again. Here were the people who, with their courage and arrogance had sailed around the world exchanging brightly-coloured beads for the breadfruit and coconuts and bananas which they coveted, and then assured the people that, in the name of his or her Britannic majesty, they could relieve them of the responsibility of defending their lands. Now they have the empire upon which the sun never sets. Rule Britannia.

Yes, here we are in London again – Exciting, overcrowded and dangerous, it will always act as a magnet for some of us. The heart beats a little faster. We would surely be missing a large slice of life if we were to leave this giant octopus.

It wouldn't be long before I settled down again.

Chapter 25

1944

We had been at war for five years; dramatic years in the history of the world and a long time in our young lives. I looked back over the time since I left school prematurely in the first spring of the war. Like so many more, I had grown up to a background of bombs and guns; accepting a scarcity of every commodity which past, and especially future generations would consider essential. We had existed on a diet which was just about adequate for our good health.

How would all this affect us in years to come, I wondered. Were we going to be cheese-paring and frugal. Already we were expected to re-use envelopes to assist the war effort. We ironed paper bags so that they could be used again. We were told to bath in five inches of water. We wasted nothing – nothing at all. Would we ever be able to take food for granted? Would this be the war to end wars?

'This time we must all make certain
That this time is the last time....'

We sang, convinced that no one would be crazy enough to go through all this again. But they said that in 1918, didn't they? Oh well, this time we meant it.

I thought of the people I'd met in the last five years. People I would never meet again. They were all part of the drama of war. And there were the friends who had shared all the dangers and who would be my friends as long as we lived. Then there's the man I married a few months ago. Would I always think of him as the wild young fellow who had learnt to make love in Spain during the civil war, who had swept German mines from the North Sea in the bitter winter of 1940, who had escorted the men who brought home the bacon in spite of the U-boats and who had found a few hours to marry me in Liverpool. Would I remember the pain of separation and the joys of reunion? Would I love him for the rest of my life?

For good or evil, the war had made an indelible impression on all our lives.

Cynthia came in and interrupted my reverie.

"I've just been thinking of all that's happened since we met."

"Yes, they've been memorable years, haven't they? I'll always remember arriving at the Goldsmith Club. It was a filthy night in December and I wondered why I'd come to London. Of course it was before the blitz. That common room was pleasant enough, but there were so many strange faces and no one was interested in the new girl until I looked at you and you gave me a big wide smile. I thought, well, there's one human being here and I felt better. I was pleased when I discovered that my room was next to yours."

Chapter 25 – 1944

"That's nice to hear. I'm glad I made you feel at home," I said. "I arrived out of a snow storm. I'd walked up from Mornington Crescent underground after a meal in Lyons Corner House in Coventry Street. The room looked bright and inviting after the terrible night outside. I'd even been approached by an old hag in the blackout. She cackled something unintelligible into my face and frightened the life out of me. I was so relieved to feel the warmth of that room. Someone was playing the piano and I thought they all looked pleasant. I was happy about the place.

"Lyn and our Scottish friend, Anne Gellatly, were friendly from the start. Then you arrived, a Welsh girl, to complete our quartet – English, Irish, Scottish and Welsh. Strange how we four got together. It seems a long time ago now. Anne is going to marry her Canadian you know."

"Any sign of Paul coming back?" I asked.

"None, I'm afraid. I have a feeling he'll be in the Pacific for the rest of the war," she said.

"Jack is still expecting to be sent out there. I hope he won't be. I was just about to make a cup of tea and I smuggled a half-bottle of Jameson back with me. That's Irish whiskey in case you don't know. A spoonful or two is good in tea. Will you join me?"

The conversation inevitably turned to what we would do after the war. Cynthia would be going to Australia as soon as Paul was demobbed. She would be half a world away. Anne would be in Canada. My future would depend on where Jack went, unless I got pregnant in the meantime. I hoped I would, but I had the feeling that Jack was in no hurry to take on the responsibility of a family.

Cynthia was just leaving when there was an earth-shattering crash.

"I wonder where that one fell," I said.

"I'm sorry for them, but I hope it will be the last tonight. I'm sleepy."

The strain of the long-drawn-out war was affecting, not only the troops, but civilians as well. It was bad enough for us, but surely it must be much worse for the Germans. Their troops were retreating all over the place and the air raids must be intolerable. Hitler had reinstated von Rundstedt to command the army and to stop the Allied advance at all costs. He might as well try to stop the incoming tide now. The situation was obviously becoming desperate for them. Where prisoners-of-war were taken there were usually very young boys among them now.

At home we knew that the bomber crews were suffering most. The prolonged sorties over enemy territory, where they were under constant attack, were proving too much for some. Psychiatric casualties among them far outnumbered those of the fighter crews. I heard some sad stories from my friend Anne Gellatly who had been nursing all through the war. Where there was a family history of mental illness, the risk of breakdown was, of course, that much greater. In many ways, these were the most tragic victims of the war.

Chapter 25 – 1944

By now we recognised the preliminaries to an invasion, the heavy bombing and shelling prior to a sea or airborne attack. Early in October, it was the Dutch island of Walcheron. The bombing went on day after day. They weren't going to make another costly mistake like Arnhem. This time they would destroy all the German strong points before they went in. Then at last they would have a foothold on Dutch soil.

Already the Allied governments which had operated from London throughout the war years, were beginning to return. The Belgians were the first to go home.

Roosevelt had started discussions with Churchill on their countries' position in Europe after the war. Churchill demanded the first say over Greece since, in his opinion, Britain must be the leading power in the Mediterranean. Roosevelt, however, was urging him to speed up the process of decolonisation, which he was reluctant to do. He had not become the king's first minister, he said, to preside over the dissolution of the British Empire.

At the same time, the Americans were advancing towards the German frontier and, early in October, had encircled the city of Aachen. In the Far East they were engaged in the greatest sea battle of the war, maybe the greatest sea battle of all time. They had captured Leyte and were determined to take the Philippines. They faced the entire Japanese fleet and, after three days of fighting, had sunk thirty-six Japanese warships. It was some compensation for Pearl Harbour.

In Italy, Canadian troops had made history by 'Crossing the Rubicon', while from Germany, we heard that Rommel, the hero of Hitler's war in the desert, had chosen to commit suicide rather than face trial. He was suspected of having been involved in the plot against the Fuehrer the previous summer.

Everything now pointed to an early Allied victory. It was just a question of time. So why did I feel depressed? For five years we had buoyed ourselves up for the daily challenges which the war brought. I had felt cheerful, even excited at times. At no time had I felt unable to cope. Now I felt deflated and I couldn't understand it. Looking back I remember the first difficult year of the war. That was the period of the 'Phoney War' when London was waiting and Hitler's worst efforts were directed against the Navy.

I was certainly upset and very disappointed at the start. I had hoped to travel for a few years before I settled down and the sudden change from peacetime was hard to take. All my plans had gone awry and we were faced with a dangerous and uncertain future. That was when my weight dropped to just over six stone and it remained around that figure for the rest of the war. I had been affected at the beginning, but it didn't make sense to feel low now. I would, no doubt, be alright when Jack got back.

Endless stories of bravery and endurance followed those early days, but in the end it was obvious that victory would be a question of economics. Russian manpower and the powerful tanks for which Hitler had no answer and, above all, American resources would defeat Germany. It was going to take more than courage to win this war.

But we would always remember those who had died in the Battle of Britain that we might live; those who were still dying to save us from flying bombs and rockets and, among them, above all we would think of the boys we had known when they were full of life and laughter.

John Pudney had written for us all in one of his most poignant war poems:

Fetch out no shroud
for Johnnie in the cloud
And keep your tears
for him in after years.

Better by far
for Johnnie the bright star,
To keep your head
And see his children fed.

A Nightingale Sang

Chapter 26

1944

October was over when a letter came from Jack. It had been written a few months earlier and his mind was obviously not on the U-boats which might be lying in wait for them. He was remembering our wedding night – our last night together.

'Tonight I'm on the middle watch, between midnight and 4 a.m., and I'm thinking of you' he wrote.

"It's only a week since I held you in my arms, but out here that's like a wild dream. I'm lonely for you. This blacked-out ship is full of ghosts and there is a loneliness which you couldn't imagine in teeming London. It's hard to remember the soft sweet smell of a girl in your arms."

There was a whole lot more. Not surprising in the circumstances. It was the sort of letter Jack wrote after midnight on the ocean.

In London it was hard to picture the Atlantic on a night in wartime. In spite of thousands of violent deaths in the last five years, there was no room for ghosts in London. Spirituality got short shrift in this worldly city. Jack was right, I couldn't imagine what life was like out there.

"I want to go on writing just to feel a little closer to you," he had written. The letter was making me sad. I could see the lonely years stretching ahead for both of us. As he said, "a few days together and then months, maybe years, apart". Oh well, I knew what I was doing. He was the man I wanted and would always want, I believed. When the war is over, who knows what chances we may get to be together.

Shortly after the letter arrived there was a telephone call from Liverpool.

"How's Mrs. Conway?"

"Jack! I've just had your letter. It took ages."

"And I've just had yours. It took even longer. Can you come up here tomorrow? I've forgotten what it feels like to kiss you and we have so little time."

"Of course I'll come. I'll be on the usual train."

Jack was at the station with the ship's little mongrel, Judy. It was great to have his arms around me again and I was in no hurry to enquire about the dog.

"The little pest," Jack said. "It's impossible to get away without her. She's running up and down the fo'c'sle, peering through the guardrail and whining. I thought I'd got away, but when looked round there she was trotting behind me. And she's just had pups again. As soon as the gangway was lowered in St. Johns, she was down. It was funny. There was a big St. Bernard on the quayside and when this one appeared, cocky as ever, the big fellow opened his jaws and clamped them across her back. She was completely shocked. It should have taught her a lesson."

Chapter 26 – 1944

"You never learn, do you? She climbed back on the gangway with her tail between her legs, but within hours she was back down again and, as usual, she was pregnant when we left. Six of the men have gone home with her pups."

"You're incorrigible," he said to the dog. "We've kept one pup for her in the hope that she'll behave herself for a while. I'll have to leave her at the Devonshire. Some of the crew will be in later."

I was relieved. She amused me, but I didn't particularly want to have to look after her.

"She won't be put out for long," Jack said. "She followed us into a dark little quayside pub in Cornwall once and the landlord gave her a saucer of beer. She always expected that, and she was lapping away happily when this voice called out, "Hello". The tone startled her, but when she looked up and saw that it came from the birdcage, she took off as if all the devils in hell were after her."

We took Judy to the Devonshire. It was one of my favourite pubs anywhere, and the lovely blazing fire tempted us to stay for a couple of drinks. Then the landlord kindly offered to look after our charge until some of the crew turned up.

Jack and I spent the night in the Royal George, as usual, and, although Jack had to leave early, he sent one of the men in for me later so that I could have a drink on board. That ended in a little jam session before we returned to town.

Put a covey of Celts together and you'll have music, and memories in the years to come. So it was then. We tried to crowd a lifetime into every meeting.

In town, we called to the pub to thank the landlord for taking care of Judy and we spent the rest of the evening there. I sat holding Jack's hand and wishing this night could last forever. How could I let him go again. It didn't get any easier, but I knew that in my memory it would last forever. I had no doubt that these precious wartime meetings would be a bond that would keep us together for the rest of our lives.

Back in London, they were talking about the fall of Aachen. It had been completely destroyed and there had been some hope that Germany would accept defeat, but Hitler ordered that they should fight on.

In some places there was still stiff resistance to allied attacks, as at St. Die, where they had held out against a sustained American assault.

From our point of view, more powerful rocket bombs were still being tested and, although the Allies were bombing sites, they were continually moving on to new venues. The danger was far from over.

On the 7th November Franklin D. Roosevelt was elected President of the United States for a fourth term and, in London, Winston Churchill was warning that the war was not won. Not until after the last battle was won, until after the last All Clear, could we celebrate the victory.

On the 11th November, the day normally held to commemorate the First World War, Churchill and De Gaulle drove together to the Arc de Triomphe and laid a wreath on the tomb of the Unknown Soldier. On the following day the R.A.F. finally put the German battleship *Tirpitz* out of commission forever, in Tromso Fiord in Norway. For the two and a half years that she had been in Norwegian waters, she was a menace to the Russian convoys. Now, after several attempts over the years, she was totally immobilised.

As the *Tirpitz* capsized it was reported that the men could be heard singing *Deutschland über Alles*.

The announcement early in September that we had seen the last of the flying bombs turned out to be optimistic and premature. When the gun crews in the Home Counties got the measure of the V-1s, the German authorities changed their tactics and ordered that they should be transported across the Channel by plane and then launched against London, so we continued to be attacked by flying bombs, as well as rockets, through the winter of 1944. That they came in smaller numbers was due to the fact that Germany no longer had planes to spare for this particular menace. Nevertheless hundreds of people were dying in explosions every month. Late in the Autumn a hundred and sixty people were killed in New Cross Road in South London when a rocket exploded one lunch hour.

Lyn was still sleeping at the Air Ministry but, after several quiet nights, I persuaded her to join half a dozen of us who were celebrating somebody's birthday at the Lord Nelson.

"You don't have to go home," I said, "you can stay at my place."

"I'll come if we can sleep in the basement," she said.

"O.K., I'll yank the mattresses down."

"No, you can't do that. Wait till I get there and I'll help you."

"Well come over early and share my Irish stew. There'll be enough for two if I put in plenty of celery and carrots and things."

"Sure you won't be short?"

"No, I have plenty of vegetables."

We had a pleasant evening and Lyn was delighted to be with the gang again, but we weren't in bed ten minutes when the warning went, followed immediately by gunfire, lots of gunfire, and explosions. Lyn had her head under her pillow, but I could hear the gasps, "Oh, my God, oh, my God". I felt guilty, as though I was responsible for the raid. It seemed to go on for ages and I knew Lyn would not be spending a night with us again for a long time.

As well as London, Antwerp was being attacked by V-1s and V-2s. It was the Allies principal port of supply now and Hitler was determined to put it out of commission. Consequently flying bombs and rockets were exploding there night and day and thousands of people were dying. A rocket exploding at a road junction killed a few hundred people, including a number of Allied servicemen who were part of a military convoy which happened to be passing.

Chapter 26 – 1944

Although there was no doubt about the fate of Nazi Germany at this point, Hitler had planned one more major offensive against the Allies before Christmas. He chose the Ardennes, where the German army had had a decisive victory against the French back in 1940. No doubt the superstitious Führer thought of it as a good omen.

On the 17th December, a quarter of a million men of the German army were massed for what became known as the Battle of the Bulge, the last great battle of the war in Europe. For once, British Intelligence had let them down. They had no advance knowledge of Hitler's intention. It took some time to realise the seriousness of the attack and for ten days the Germans advanced and encircled thousands of American troops, who were forced to surrender.

At that point, General Eisenhower put Montgomery in command of the whole operation. The Americans were bearing the brunt of the offensive and were called on by the Germans to surrender, to which the American commander replied in one word, "Nuts!".

It was into the first week of January before the Allies had Hitler's army in retreat in the Ardennes, and another two weeks before German withdrawal was complete. Their last major offensive was costly in terms of men and materials.

A Nightingale Sang

Chapter 27

1944-1945

A couple of weeks before Christmas I had a telephone call from my brother. He was now a quantity surveyor with Wimpey, one of the biggest construction companies in the country and, like thousands of other young Irishmen, he was busy rebuilding England.

Patrick was spending Christmas in Oswestry in Shropshire with friends and they suggested that I might like to join them. My brother, known here as Pat, had written and spoken about this family several times since his arrival in England and I was sure a visit to Oswestry would be a lot of fun.

I travelled north the day before Christmas Eve and was immediately involved in a social whirl. There were two girls in the Hughes family, one recently married, and they had a host of friends in this small town on the Welsh border. All the boys were in the services, but one of them, David, known as Spike, was home on Christmas leave from the Navy, so I had a partner for dancing and an escort for the various parties.

"How about a climb in the Berwyn Mountains tomorrow," Julie said after Christmas dinner, when we were all in need of fresh air and exercise.

"That's a great idea," Spike said, and it was decided that Pat and Julie and Spike and I would leave early the following morning. Like the other boys I'd known, Spike's father had saved his petrol ration so that his boys on leave could use his car. Anyway the trip turned out to be a lot more exciting than we had intended.

We started out early and reached the peak in good time. We ate sandwiches and washed them down with a handful of pure white snow. Then we started down the mountain in fine fettle. Sadly, half way down Julie tripped and sprained her ankle badly. We rested for a while hoping it would recover sufficiently for her to hobble. No such luck, so the boys made a chair with their hands and we proceeded very slowly until we came to a rock which gave some shelter from the wind.

"Frances, you and I should carry on down now as fast as we can and get the Rescue Services out," Spike said.

The light was already fading, but the track stood out dark against the surrounding snow-covered ground, so we made good time and found the people with the stretchers.

"Don't tell me you were so bloody stupid as to go up there in December without torches or whistles," one man said to Spike.

Chapter 27 – 1944/1945

"I'm afraid we were," Spike said humbly. Heaven forbid that we would sound cocky. "Do you want me to come back with you?" he added.

"Yes, you'd better," the man said. He wasn't going to let him off the hook. I wasn't to be included in the rescue party. Who said it was a man's' world?

They were back in an hour or so. Julie had her ankle bandaged and she was feeling better. We all made our way to the village pub and drank hot whiskies. The musicians came in later and Welsh hospitality was not found wanting. It was a great night and we decided that we were in no fit state to drive home.

I won't forget my first night in the Welsh mountains. In fact, the whole Christmas visit was a huge success and, as Oswestry was reasonably close to Liverpool, I was planning to suggest to Jack that we should come back some time soon.

I was really sorry to leave Oswestry and my new friends. It was so good to be away from the war for a while.

When I got back they told me there had been a flying bomb attack on Christmas Eve and, as well as high explosives, the bombs had carried Christmas greetings from the prisoners-of-war. These were strewn like confetti around the countryside. The men had been surprised to be allowed another letter home before Christmas. They had no idea how they were to be delivered.

1945

So here we are at the start of another year of war and, as with every New Year, and Christmas too, I found myself remembering the past.

I had spent the Christmas of 1939, the first Christmas of the war, at the Goldsmith Club and I can still hear the pretty Czechoslovakian girl making a speech of thanks on behalf of her friends, in her lovely broken English. She reminded us of how they had been forced to choose between leaving home or living under a Nazi regime. She was grateful to England and to the Goldsmith Club for making them welcome. We found the Czech girls delightful company.

Another outstanding memory from that sad Christmas was the radio programme from the troops in France. The graphic picture of men on a poplar-lined road, accompanied by the sound of marching feet, was so real that it is with me still. The blacked-out stations and couples clasped in a last farewell were still new to us then and they made a deep impression. The early days of the war were depressing.

For the following three years I wore a maple leaf on my shoulder. Those were the Sandy years of air raids, and loving memories.

New Year of 1944 was Hogmanay when I was in Scotland with Joe Loss.

What eventful years they had all been, following the changing fortunes of the Allies, making and losing friends, from a schoolgirl at the beginning to a married woman now. These will surely be years of outstanding memories in all our lives.

What surprises will 1945 hold for the world? Will we celebrate the end of the war at last, or will the Japanese be able to hold out for another year? Will Jack be going to the Far East, and where is he now? There have been too many heartaches, too many shattered lives. Let's hope 1945 will bring happiness and peace back to this war-torn world.

It was better that we didn't know that New Year's Day in 1945 that ninety-five Allied prisoners-of-war were killed accidentally by Allied bombers while repairing the Burma-Thailand railway of death, where they had suffered so much during the years of its construction.

That January President Roosevelt announced that the number of Americans killed, or missing presumed killed, since Pearl Harbour was more than two hundred thousand, and Winston Churchill gave the number of British and Commonwealth servicemen killed as over a quarter of a million.

However, one event which gave us real pleasure that January was the departure of a boat train from Victoria Station in London bound for Paris. It was the first London-Paris train since May 1940. It had always been exciting seeing Le Train

Bleu leaving Victoria for the French Riviera and it was great to know that we could look forward to seeing it again.

With the surrender of Budapest to the Russians on the 18th January, several capital cities which had been occupied by the Nazis were now in Allied hands. They included Rome, Warsaw, Paris, Brussels, Athens, Belgrade, and now Budapest, but over much of Europe prisoners-of-war were on the march now. Ahead of the Allied advance they were being removed from the camps and joining the prisoners from notorious camps like Auschwitz and Belsen who were also being ousted by the Germans. In bitter cold, and suffering from starvation, they were being pushed beyond endurance and many were dying by the roadside.

At home, the black-out rules were being relaxed to some extent. In fact, Chelsea, which still had gaslights, probably to show its individuality, was now allowed street lamps. So, on a visit to a local pub we no longer needed our blacked-out torches. All torches had a black disc over the bulbs from which a small cross had been cut, to give limited light. The same principal applied to the traffic lights, which showed green, amber or red crosses throughout the war. Of course, leaving Chelsea, the blacked-out districts seemed ever darker.

I was sitting at home one evening trying to read when there was a telephone call from Lyn.
"I'm fed up," she said. "Will you come to the Overseas Club? We haven't been there for ages."

"Yes, sure. I'm dying for a dance and some music. I'm just in the mood to jitterbug to 'Pennsylvania 6-5000', or, heaven, swing to 'Lady be Good' … well, maybe not that one. I'm glad you rang. I'm feeling restless".

"Well, I must admit I hadn't thought of anything more than a drink," she said.

"Yeah, that too. Talk about 'Don't get around much anymore', I was even wishing it was fire-watching night. I'll meet you at the Club."

Lyn was already there when I arrived and I went up to the bar and got what closely resembled a gin and orange juice. I was immediately joined by an American lieutenant.

"Let me get that," he said.

"Thank you," I said, "but he's already taken my money." The newcomer looked quite nice and I did want to dance. He came to our table.

"Do you mind if we join you?" He called his friend over.

"If you're not going to be bored with two old married ladies," I said.

Lyn said nothing. Time enough to decide whether she wanted to remain single.

"Would you like to dance," the first one said to me.

"I would love to, as a matter of fact," I said, and, like most of the Americans I'd met, he could certainly move on the dance floor. He told me he was of Polish extraction. His name was Witold, but in the army he was known as Joe.

We danced again and again and, in between, I took little sips of my drink. Alarm bells were ringing and I wasn't going to be plied with drink. Lyn and I were not going home together. I wouldn't dare to ask her to come back to Chelsea in case there was a raid.

"Is Lyn your room-mate?" Joe asked.

"No, my room-mate didn't want to come out tonight," I lied.

The band was playing. 'I don't want to set the world on fire', and I was singing along.

"You don't have to set the world on fire, but is there any need to be so darned frigid?" he said.

I was rapidly going off this guy.

We returned to our table and I gave Lyn a quizzical look, but she smiled happily at her companion, so I took it that I was free to go.

"I think I'd better be going Lyn," I said. "I've come without a key and I don't want to have to wake my friend up."

"Am I going to be allowed to take you home?" Joe said.

"Not tonight," I said, "but thank you for some great dancing."

He wasn't pleased but, as they say, you can't win 'em all.

Chapter 28

1945

Throughout January the German army was in retreat. They destroyed the gas chambers and crematoria at Auschwitz just ahead of the Russian advance. The liberators were in time to save the Italian, Primo Levi, who would become a Nobel Laureate.

Surprisingly, the Germans were still capable of counterattacking in a few places, such as the French town of Colmar where the actor, Lieutenant Audi Murphy, was wounded. Later he would take the part of himself in the film 'To Hell and Back'.

They wanted the women's' services overseas now, and one of the first to volunteer was Churchill's daughter, Mary, a Junior Commander, equal to the rank of captain. All two hundred and thirty women under her command, volunteered as well.

At this point they were asking for volunteers, but the Prime Minister was of the opinion and if they didn't have enough volunteers, they would have to make it a directive.

I had given very little thought to joining any of the services up to now, but I was beginning to wonder about applying to the WRNS. It was the hardest service to get into, but I wouldn't have the slightest interest in any of the others.

All through the dark winter days of 1945, the Russian army was advancing on Berlin. There was every reason to believe that they would be the first of the Allies to reach the capital of Hitler's Germany. But, long before this time, Roosevelt had expressed to Churchill his earnest hope that the Western Allies would capture Berlin, or at least enter the city at the same time as the Russians.

Several matters were outstanding in the early days of the new year, and it was time for the leaders to meet. Yalta on the Black Sea, was chosen as the venue, but Churchill arranged to meet Roosevelt in Malta before they spoke to Stalin. He was the Uncle Joe, or UJ, of their correspondence. Presumably none of them realised at that time how very ill and close to death the American President was. Churchill seemed to be the last to see how frail the man was. He even made the remark in Yalta that Roosevelt was taking no interest in what they were trying to do.

One of Churchill's main concerns was a new type of U-boat which had sunk twelve ships in the Atlantic recently. There was, as yet, no deterrent for it, but they knew that many of them were being built at Danzig and he stressed to Stalin the hope that the Russians would capture the port before long.

Chapter 28 - 1945

On the 13th February, while Churchill was still abroad, the R.A.F. carried out one of the most controversial air raids of the war, that of the destruction of the city of Dresden. The American Air Force followed the night raid with another the following day and Dresden was left in smouldering ruins. This was said to be the result of an agreement with Stalin to prevent German reinforcements getting through to the Eastern front.

At the same time, fourteen V-2 rockets had fallen on London. Jack had rung the night before to say that he would be able to spend a few days in London and would catch an early train the next morning. It would mean that I could spend the whole weekend with him. I was wildly excited. I had missed him so much. I wanted to dance again, and make love.

Joe Loss was playing in Hammersmith and I suggested that we should go there on his first night home. 'It had to be you', 'You'd be so nice to come home to', 'As time goes by', one after the other we danced, until Jack insisted on stopping for a drink and for a while we sat on the balcony holding hands and watching the dancers.

"Come on, let's go home," Jack said then, and we went to collect our coats.

The mens' cloakroom was upstairs and I was standing in the foyer, amused at the eagerness of the servicemen coming downstairs. I was wondering whether Jack would be in such a hurry. I needn't have had any doubts. He came whistling and running, two steps at a time. I was laughing when he joined me.

"What's funny?" he said.

"I was wondering if you were going to be as keen as the rest to get down here."

"Are you kidding?" he said, sweeping me out into the street.

A couple of rockets had exploded before we left home, but I had forgotten about them, so it was a shock to hear another mighty explosion while we waited for a taxi. There were several more before the morning. Indeed it was impossible to get much sleep.

"I thought your sleepless nights were a thing of the past," Jack said. "How do you manage to work when you're awake half the night?"

"I suppose we're used to it," I said. "Anyway, there's no work tomorrow, so maybe we should go to the coast and get some fresh air. How about a walk along the cliffs at Eastbourne and a nice dinner there? The parents of one of my school friends have a hotel there. I spent my last Christmas at school with them, or with Caroline and her mother. We could spend the night there, perhaps. What do you think?"

"Sounds good to me. You could do with a rest from these rockets."

"Oh, Frances, this is terrible," Mrs. Bowers said when I rang. "You've just missed Caroline." (She called her Carol-ene in the French manner). "She'll be so disappointed. We were talking about you and your last holiday with us. What a long time ago. We had no idea then how that year would end. Caroline is at Bovington Camp in Dorset. Joan Davidge is there too. You know, of course, that her husband was killed. We look after the baby here. You'll be able to see him. He's adorable."

"Yes, I hear from Caroline occasionally. We write for Christmas and birthdays. I'll look forward to seeing the baby."

"Caroline tells me you're married."

"Yes, my husband will be coming with me. It will be lovely to see you again. You were the first one to suggest cutting my long hair."

"We had to try and make you look grown up, didn't we? We'll be delighted to have you with us for a few days."

"You'll love this place," I said to Jack. "It's on the white cliffs overlooking the English Channel. It's called The Lighthouse and the whole theme is maritime. It was damaged by bombs during the Battle of Britain, but they've managed to keep going.

"Caroline's father was in the Secret Service during the First World War and he married her mother in France when she was seventeen. I think it was a stormy marriage. They were separated when we were at school, although he used to visit. The Christmas I was there, they would have loud arguments in French, even when he took us out for drives. Caroline's mother is gorgeous and she had plenty of admirers, but now, it seems, they're back together again.

"I had my first real drink with them – Gin and Italian Vermouth, Gin and It to the cognoscenti. It was a fashionable drink then. I was also tempted to try smoking when I saw the black, gold tipped cigarettes Mrs. Bowers smoked through a long elegant cigarette-holder. I soon got tired of that. They were too expensive anyway, but it was a great holiday, one I'll never forget."

We had a wonderful few days. I had some pastels with me and was tempted to do some drawing when I saw a lone airman walking at the foot of Beachy Head. I think it could be called Magic Realism. When I thought of friends who had gone, it somehow looked Otherworldly."

Coming back in the train, I said to Jack, "I'm probably pregnant."

"Well, that's what you want, isn't it? Actually, I thought that baby suited you!"

"Would you mind?"

"It might as well be now as later, I suppose. You could go back to Ireland if you liked. I'm sure it would be the best thing, especially if I have to go to the Pacific."

"Oh, don't think about that. Anyway we'll have to wait and see."

Jack caught an early train in the morning and this time I felt that I would be seeing him again soon, in spite of Hitler's new U-boats which could stay under water for ages, it seemed. He would almost certainly be going on another Atlantic convoy, which would mean being back in Liverpool in the early days of the summer.

Chapter 28 - 1945

We had both been fascinated by the Bower's hotel and its position on the cliff facing the European battleground. It would be easy to imagine the ghost of the old sea captain who had owned the original house before the Bowers extended it. I pictured him at the top window peering into his telescope. What would he think of this mammoth twentieth-century struggle? Had he been engaged in sea battles in his time? Was he at The Nile with Nelson, I wonder?

All the myriad craft that had sailed that summer five years ago to rescue the men from Dunkirk, what a sight they must have been from The Lighthouse. I never tired of listening to Mrs. Bowers' accounts of the events of the last several years. Even over the weekend we spent there, we had watched wave after wave of bombers on their destructive missions.

It was an amazing house and I intended to go back there as soon as I could, this time on my own, with my paints. Maybe I'd get a glimpse of the bearded mariner pacing the white cliffs. For now, it was back to reality, but first I had to write and tell Caroline about or few magic days with her son and her parents. I hadn't seen her for ages and there was not much likelihood of her spending time in London when she could be with her baby. We would have to rely on correspondence.

A last air raid to destroy all German communications was in progress now. We heard that thousands of planes were involved against railways, bridges and road transport. It covered a wide area, and resulted in one pilot being awarded a posthumous Victoria Cross. The South African, Captain Swales, managed to keep his damaged plane in the air long enough for his crew to parachute to safety. He was killed when the plane crashed.

The Red Army was closing in on Berlin and, from all accounts, everyone in the city would be expected to build trenches and tank traps. Unlike Rome and Paris, which had been declared 'Open' and undefended, Berlin would be a fortress.

On the Western Front, the Canadians had forced the Germans back across the Upper Rhine, where 22,000 of them were taken prisoner, and in the Far East the Americans were fighting to take Iwo Jima Island in Tokyo Bay. Many thousands of them would die there before their air base could be established.

Early in the war, people were cheered up with the silly little song 'We're going to hang out the washing on the Siegried Line'. It didn't happen then, but now, five and a half years later, the outer defences of this great fortification had been breached by the Americans. How our lives had changed since that time. The post-war world would be a very different place to the one we had known.

On the 14th March, the papers headlined that the flamboyant General 'Blood and Guts' Patton had sent a signal, "Today I peed in the Rhine", and, by the 23rd March the

Chapter 28 - 1945

Canadians and Americans were massed on a wide front preparing to cross the river in force.

It will never be known how many men, women and children had died before the war reached this stage. The Soviet Union alone could claim to have lost twenty million citizens and the Jews counted their losses at about six million.

I was feeling weary and longing for the sea and the country again so I decided to have a weekend out of London. As well as the rockets, we were having to contend with the airborne flying bombs, and the nights were still likely to be disturbed by the sirens. By this time I knew that I was pregnant and I was terrified of doing anything wrong, so I decided to ask the doctor's advice about going away. He laughed when I told him I was four weeks pregnant and told me to go off and enjoy myself.

I decided to visit my old school in Wimborne, to call on one of the girls I still wrote to in Bournemouth and, maybe, to see Caroline Bowers and Joan Davidge. It would be a busy weekend.

I enjoyed the train ride through vaguely familiar country. It brought back memories of the day I travelled with my mother, a small twelve-year-old, new to England and everything English. 'You are now in the Strong Country' said the large signs advertising Strong and Company Ales. Then, the Brooklands Motor Racing track, presumably unused since the war. The years slipped away.

It was a sunny Sunday afternoon when I first saw the lovely old house which was to be my home for the next five years. Joan Davidge was the girl who came through the French doors to welcome me to St. Cuthburga's. We sat on the bank above the tennis courts while she told me about the school. A local Anglo-Saxon martyr had given it its name, she said.

The school was a comparatively small one, set in beautiful gardens among the Dorset pinewoods. The day pupils came from the local town, a market town for the rich farmland of East Dorset. The boarders were mostly Londoners, whose parents were in the colonial service in Africa and India, although Joan, and one or two others, came from Bournemouth, or nearby. I can see her still, dressed for the weekend in her yellow angora sweater. Now she was in the army and I looked forward to seeing her again.

On my arrival I was invited to have supper with the seniors who were, maybe, ten or eleven years old when I had last seen them. Afterwards, I spent the evening at the Kings Head in the town with Barbara Deane, a friend from the old days.

"Have you kept up your dancing?" she wanted to know. She and I had taken our dancing very seriously at school.

"Not really," I said. "I danced in a stage show at home once, and afterwards the nuns from the local convent and several mothers asked me to take classes. I did for a while, but I wanted to get back to London. I believe you've been teaching here."

"Yes, I still take classes, and I'm very disappointed to hear that you've given it up. You enjoyed it so much."

"I did, and I still enjoy ballroom dancing and anything that passes for ballroom dancing these days, but honestly after school I wanted to be with grown-ups. I didn't care much for teaching – maybe later on, but I'm pregnant now anyway."

"Lucky you. I wish I was, but my husband has been overseas since the second year of the war. I married out of dancing school and he was sent away almost immediately afterwards."

"That's awful. I'm so sorry."

"It is awful, and now I'm not sure whether I want him back. We've both grown up and changed. I'm sure, and now I've met someone else. I haven't written a 'Dear John' yet, but I haven't written anything else either, not for a long time. My father is angry about it, but my mother is more understanding. It's bloody, this war, isn't it?"

"Yes, it is. It's been hard on everyone and it's not our fault," I said.

"You don't want to stay in this place tonight, do you? Come and stay with me. We can have a good old natter. You'll be doing me a favour. I get fed up on my own."

So I spent the night with Barbara, and in the morning I caught the Hants and Dorset bus to Bournemouth. I laughed to myself when I remembered how at school we used to call it the Pants and Corset. What else would schoolgirls call it?

Caroline and Joan had arranged to come to Bournemouth where we were to meet another of our old friends, but first I was anxious to take a long walk on the promenade above Bournemouth's lovely beach, to remind me of some of our happiest days at school. Bournemouth was heaven to us then.

I had booked to stay at the Branksome Towers. It was the only hotel I could remember by name and now I had to take a taxi to meet the girls there. They arrived in the height of good humour, which was a relief after my sad friend in Wimborne. They were both in uniform and Caroline looked gorgeous as ever. We sat in the bar with drinks, where Lorna joined us. It was really exciting seeing them all again and we all talked together, making so much noise that we attracted the attention of some Polish airmen, who made no attempt to disguise their interest, so we decided to move into the dining room, drinks and all.

"I've seen your beautiful son," I said to Caroline.

"He's angelic, isn't he?" she said. "So sad that his father never saw him. You know, even the day we were married, the vicar talked about the number of pilots who had been killed. I was in tears at my wedding."

"That was a strange thing for the clergyman to do," I said.

"Yes, but she's practically engaged again," Joan said. "She can have anyone."

"He's very anxious to get married," Caroline said. "I feel as though I'm being rushed." I'm not that keen to risk it all again with another airman. It's just that he was so sympathetic when Mark was killed. I needed him then."

"Only you can decide that one," I said.

"You said you were pregnant," Joan said, and they all laughed when they knew it was only a month since Jack had been home.

"There's many a slip ...." Joan said.

"No, no, I'm definitely pregnant," I said. I didn't want to have any doubts about it.

"Make sure you have a girl," Lorna said. "I have any amount of baby clothes left from my two-year-old. You won't need any coupons."

That would be a great help of course, but I was looking forward to making everything myself, although I didn't say so. Instead I said, "Have you all forgotten that this is St. Patrick's Day? Do you remember how we used to celebrate it at school? I wonder if they still get up at four o'clock in the morning to sing Irish songs?"

"I wonder," Lorna said. "Do you still sing, Fran?"

"Every chance I get," I said.

"What I liked was breaking that awful Lenten fast," Caroline said. "We used to gorge on sweets that day. I still feel guilty about eating a sweet in Lent. These things affect one for ever, I suppose, and I'm not even a Catholic. You are, Frances, how do you feel?"

"Oh, I still try to give up alcohol. This year was easy. I'm sticking to soft drinks now."

"At least you'll be getting real orange juice while you're pregnant. That's something."

"Yes, I can make jelly out of it sometimes, but there'll be no cream or ice cream. We've all forgotten the taste of those things."

"Hey, look at the time," Joan said suddenly. "We'll miss that train," and the two girls rushed away. I wondered when we would all meet again.

Chapter 29

1945

It was almost over, this war that had broken hearts and homes; had taught us more about life and love, hatred and revenge in its six years, than we could otherwise have learnt in several lifetimes. Now we were definitely coming to the end. Nobody knew when, but all the signs were that we could count the months on one hand. My baby would be born into a world at peace again, and for that I would be eternally grateful.

According to the news on the 23rd March, General Patton had crossed the Rhine at Oppenheim. On the same night, the British and Canadian forces crossed the Rhine, blinding the German defenders with their brilliantly illuminated tanks, known as 'Monty's Moonlight', and in the Far East British and Indian troops had taken Mandalay.

Now I decided to see my doctor about the pregnancy. I took the morning off and was preparing to go out when there was an explosion somewhere nearby. The shutters on my big front window clattered shut as the glass shattered and I was thrown against the mantelpiece. Apart from a bruise over one eye, I was not hurt, just a bit shaken. The bruise was tender to touch, but the skin was not broken, so I made a cup of tea and sat down to recover before I rang Lou about the window. I didn't think there was any harm done, but I would mention it to the doctor anyway.

My G.P. confirmed that I was pregnant and suggested that I should take the day off. Otherwise I should be alright, he said.

We didn't know it then, but this was one of the last rockets to fall on London. In all, since the previous September, almost three thousand people had been killed by V-2s in the capital, and now, at last, the troops on the continent had been able to bomb the launching sites out of existence.

By the end of March, we had also seen the last of the flying bombs. Seven thousand five hundred had been launched since the previous June. They had destroyed twenty-five thousand houses and killed over six thousand people in London. It was hard to believe now that we were to have peaceful nights for the first time in ages.

On the continent, the Americans were building new bridges and strengthening existing bridges over the Rhine and all the Allied armies were advancing in one direction. Their destination was Berlin.

> *'This time we will not say curtains*
> *Till we ring them down in their own home town.'*

We had sung the song and danced to the music for the last three years. Now it was almost a reality and, while the generals marched together towards the ever-advancing Soviets, the politicians worried about the after-effects. It was obvious that the Russians intended to be the first into Berlin and Churchill was worried, fearful that a Communist regime would be established in the conquered areas after the war.

The situation in Poland was particularly worrying because the free elections vouched for at the Yalta Conference would not now take place there, but in America Roosevelt was dying and the British Prime Minister could no longer expect his support in his opposition to Stalinist policy.

It wasn't only the politicians who worried about the Eastern Allies. One man I knew wrote and sealed, and locked in his desk, his post-war prophecy.

"You know what I've written here," he said. I didn't.

"When this is over, we will unite with Germany to defeat the Soviet Union."

"What about our 'Rushen' office boy," I said facetiously. It happened to be the lad's name. "I wonder what he takes out in his Wellingtons?"

My friend didn't approve of any attitude.

Budapest had surrendered to the Russians after a stiff fight, but now they continued their advance towards the Austrian border. They would be the first into Vienna.

Our immediate concern at home was a notice in the papers that potatoes might have to be rationed. I wondered how the British Restaurants would cope. They had been set up early in the war and their main fare was known as S.O.P., Sausages (made mainly of bread), onions and potatoes. Their prices were rock-bottom to ensure that no one need go without a hot meal at least once a day. It was vital to keep the nation healthy and, in fact, absenteeism was never lower than during the war years. But there was a shortage of potatoes at this time and, although the fish and chip shops could often provide fish, it was necessary in some areas to bring your own potatoes. They had no objection to frying them for customers.

In fact, potato rationing never became a reality, which was just as well for me because potato cakes, rissoles and fish cakes were an acceptable part of my diet.

On the Wednesday before Easter I had a telephone call from Lyn.

"Why don't we get out of London for the weekend?" she said. "We'll be off work from Thursday evening until Tuesday morning. I'd love a breath of country air."

"I think that's a great idea, and I'm sure Cynthia would like to come. Have you any place in mind?"

"I was hoping you'd suggest some place," she said.

"What about the Peak District?" I said. "Have you been there?" She hadn't.

"Well, before the war, the weather was like this and I had a lovely holiday up there. It's beautiful. That time we travelled overnight to Derbyshire and arrived in the Peaks as the sun was rising. I'll always remember that morning,

although I'd rather not travel overnight now. We could leave
early on the Friday. What do you think? Do you still belong to
the Youth Hostel Association? There are some nice hostels
up there."

"That would be fine," she said.
"We could stay at Dovedale," I said, "or, if you'd like to
climb, we could stay near Kinder Scout. It's lovely country."
"Can I leave it to you, and ask Cynthia."

So we travelled north on Good Friday morning. We
spent the days walking and the nights in Youth Hostels. We
joined up with a few young people who had guitars and
enjoyed singing. Among the songs we learned was a rousing
number from the American Revolution, which appealed to my
rebellious soul as well as to my Welsh Nationalist friend,
Cynthia, who played the flute. It became one of our favourite
duets over the following weeks.

'When America drew breath,
It was Liberty or death'

We would sing with great gusto. I don't think Lyn
approved, but she didn't take us too seriously. It was a good
weekend and we returned to London on Monday night feeling
the benefit of the fresh air and freedom. We had seen no
newspapers, but on the train we heard that the Americans
had landed on Okinawa, and adopted the slogan 'Home alive
in forty-five'. There was a feeling of optimism in the air,
although the battle for Okinawa was a ferocious hand-to-hand
one where bayonets were used in close combat. There were

thousands of kamikaze attacks and more than a quarter of a million Japanese and Americans were to die before the U.S. troops could claim Okinawa.

I was feeling particularly lively and cheerful. The morning sickness I had endured seemed to be easing off and, best of all, I hadn't had a migraine for two months. It was a new lease of life and everybody had to hear that I was pregnant, everybody that is, except my husband. I believe this particular convoy was to call to Gibraltar and maybe West Africa, so it was unlikely that Jack would receive any of my letters until he returned to Liverpool. Deliveries of mail were hazardous and uncertain. The U-boats were now fitted with snorkels and more ships were going to the bottom and we could not be sure of letters getting through. We had to be grateful that so many were delivered intact. I had a few from civilian friends which looked like lacework by the time the censor had finished with his scissors, when people had been too explicit about air raids, perhaps.

In early April the Russians were already fighting in the suburbs of Vienna and were preparing for their onslaught on Berlin. Eisenhower had decided that the Western Allies would not try to take the capital, although Churchill disagreed with him.

The Americans had reached the first of the German death camps and the horror of these skeletal human beings among countless emaciated corpses so shocked the troops that Eisenhower was sent for and he telephoned Churchill to describe what they had found. It was a camp in which four thousand inmates had died, or been murdered, in recent months. The place was Ohrdruf. It was the first of the horror camps. It would not be the last.

On the 11th April the Americans reached Buchenwald Concentration Camp, but the stories of the horrific scenes there were displaced by the announcement of the death of President Roosevelt at Warm Springs, Georgia, on the 12th April. The Allies mourned the loss of the man who could be said to have been the saviour of Europe. Without his support and practical help from the earliest days of the war, and his eventual declaration of war in December 1941, there would have been a different story to tell.

Vienna fell to the Russians the day after President Roosevelt's death. Every day now we read of new conquests. On the 15th April the Canadians finally captured Arnhem, where so many had died seven months earlier. That same day Eva Braun joined Hitler in his bunker fifty feet under Berlin. She had declared that she had no wish to live in a Germany without Hitler.

On the 16th April the Red Army opened its offensive against Berlin and United States troops liberated the prisoner-of-war camp Colditz. The British took Lubeck on the Baltic in order to prevent the Russian occupation of Denmark.

To remind us all of what we had been through, Churchill told the House of Commons that, up to the previous February, sixty thousand civilians had been killed in air raids and close on two million houses had been destroyed or damaged. And now it was almost over, for us in Europe.

British troops had reached the hell-hole that was Belsen Concentration Camp. On the 19th April we had a horrific report from Richard Dimbleby. He described a skeletal girl, her facial bones covered in what looked like yellow parchment trying to plead with him for medicine. She was unable to cry. He picked his way over corpses in the gloom to where dozens of naked bodies lay piled up under the trees. It was hard to believe that they had ever been human beings. One woman, on the point of madness, flung herself at a British soldier begging for milk for her baby, a baby who had been dead for days.

"I have never seen British soldiers so moved to cold fury as the men who opened the Belsen camp this week," Dimbleby wrote.

On the 22nd April, a Russian war communiqué described Goebbels' appeal scrawled in white paint on the walls of Berlin: 'Every German will defend his capital. We shall stop the Red hordes at the walls of our Berlin'. The Russian batteries, however, were already firing on the Spree bridges and the railway stations.

The headlines of the London Evening News on the 24th April 1945 told the story. 'RUSSIANS ENTER BERLIN – First Pictures'. Berlin troops had begun to surrender, said the report, Panic and demoralisation mounting'. A white flag had been raised before hundreds of Germans appeared with their hands up. They said that central Berlin was a living hell, but many German officers were still threatening to shoot any men suggesting capitulation. We had heard that the Germans dreaded falling into Russian hands and in Berlin their worst fears were being realised. "This is the end," they said.

Most of the northern suburbs were now in Russian hands, the south-westerly escape routes had been sealed off and fighting was raging in the southern suburbs.

The Evening News also told us that Patton's flying columns had advanced eighteen miles on a twenty-five mile front in their race for Hitler's Bavarian hide-out, but Hitler had decided to stay in Berlin.

The discovery of the concentration camps where millions of Jews were exterminated, led to General Eisenhower inviting the United Nations War Crimes Commission to send representatives to investigate Buchenwald, Belsen, Auschwitz and Dachau. The British Government would be among those likely to be involved in gathering evidence against those responsible for the horrors committed in the camps. Joseph Kramer, Belsen's commandant and known as the 'Beast of Belsen', will be tried by the countries against whose subjects he committed atrocities. He is at present under close arrest in a field military camp.

A Nightingale Sang

Chapter 30

1945

London had changed. While people shared a common danger, during the Battle of Britain and through all the dangerous years that followed, British reserve gave way to a neighbourliness that may have been unknown for generations. All the glory of the Victorian and Edwardian eras never produced the fellow feeling that Hitler managed to engender during the war years.

I thought of the people who had shared these memorable years with me, especially of those who are no longer here, but decided I mustn't get sad. I had a baby to think about now. A baby in peacetime! What could be better?

We will all be looking to Japan and the Far East now, I wondered. How long will it be before that war is over? How many more will die? Will Jack have to go, I wonder. I must write to him again. I write most days, adding a little to the letter each time. It's better that way. It will be weeks before he gets the letter and I think he'd rather have one long one than several short notes. No doubt he'll be wondering whether I'm pregnant, but wherever Jack is, he'll be enjoying himself. 'All their wars are merry'. I definitely think he's one of those Irishmen.

How much do I know about the man I married? I know he's cheerful – and passionate. He has a great sense of humour and he's brave. I don't doubt that, in dangerous situations, anyone would feel better because he was there. Apart from all that I'm crazy about him. What else matters?

Harry Truman had succeeded President Roosevelt in America. He had his work cut out to follow such an inspirational leader. He made an appealing speech and we'll all be wishing him well. He'll need all his wisdom to finish the war with Japan. Time will tell how that will go and how long it will last. The raids on Tokyo are extremely heavy and thousands are dying there. It hardly seems possible that they will allow it to continue very much longer.

Before the end of the month, we heard that Mussolini had been shot dead by the Italian Resistance.

Churchill's insistence on the importance of Britain in the Mediterranean had been a thorn in the flesh of the other major powers, and his anxiety to keep the Left out of power in Greece, had aggravated some of his own people. His return to power in a post-war election might not be as cut and dried as the Tories think.

Young people were an important part of the social revolution and the new egalitarianism which the war had brought about and their vote could influence the outcome of an election in an unexpected manner. Time would tell. Areas like South Wales and north east England would want a share of the prosperity which had been taken for granted by London and the south-east. The future was full of interest. There was so much to be done.

Medical care and Education would be reviewed in this new world. A section of the community which had been unable to afford medical care and which had been denied second and third-level education would be unlikely to accept such a situation for their children – not after what they'd all been through. We would all be anxious to play a part in reforming the lot of those who had been disadvantaged. It was exciting to be young when there was so much to look forward to.

During the week when we were preparing for Lyn's wedding, the papers reported that men of the American Third Army had met up with Russian troops at Torgau, south of Berlin. Apparently there was genuine delight in the encounter and, for all of us it was another indication that the end was just around the corner.

It wasn't all plain sailing, however. While General Eisenhower and President Truman were agreeable to the Russians taking Prague, Prime Minister Churchill was anxious for the Third Army to take advantage of their proximity to the city and to press on before the Red Army. Churchill foresaw problems in the future if the Soviets accepted the surrender of the capital of Czechoslovakia.

During the day news came through that Hitler had shot himself in his bunker under Berlin, after marrying Eva Braun, his constant companion. Eva had taken poison. Both their bodies were burnt. No doubt they had heard that the Russians were only a quarter of a mile away.

Goebbels, Hitler's Propaganda Minister, poisoned his wife and six children and then shot himself.

On the 2nd May Berlin fell to the Red Army. Hitler had declared that he would never leave Berliners alone to the mercy of the Soviets, but only his ashes remained when his arch enemies took possession of his capital.

Chapter 31

1945

Now I'll think about my baby. Will it be a boy or a girl? I think it's a girl. I know I'm thinking pink. I've knitted a pink and white striped cardigan. The buttons are pink kittens – not easy to do up. I have told Jack in the letter to look for some pink material to make a pram cover. Everything is pink or white. I've nothing blue. It's bound to be a girl. Maybe I should be thinking yellow or green. A boy would be nice too. I don't mind as long as it's a baby.

If Jack can get some material, I'll look for transfers – toadstools and gnome and things. Then I can embroider or appliqué them on to the pram cover, or eiderdown. This morning I had a telephone call from Norma Baxter who was at school with me. I have spent many weekends with her and her father over the last six years and now she wants to come and stay with me for a while.

"You're very welcome to my spare divan for as long as you want to stay," I told her.
"Fran, I've got to get away from here for a week or two," she said. "I've had a letter from John to say he'll be back in England soon, and I just don't want to see him. I haven't written to him for over a year and this is the first time I've

heard from him in ages. It's all over between us. I have no feeling for him now."

Norma and John were married a month or two after the war started. She was seventeen and very much in love. John was posted overseas six weeks later and Norma was heartbroken. Within months she was suffering from anorexia and she became a shadow of the bonny girl she'd been. Her mother had died several years earlier, so an aunt in Bournemouth took care of her and nursed her back to health.

Inevitably she met someone else, which helped with her recovery and she was able to return home to Wembley. That was years ago, and John became the forgotten man, like so many others.

"Wouldn't you like to talk things over with him," I asked.

"There's nothing to talk about, Frances. It's all over – definitely. I'd like to come and stay with you."

"That's alright with me, honey. Stay as long as you like."

It was another war casualty.

I had known John, so I felt some sympathy for him. On the other hand, various snippets of information coming through indicated that he had been by no means celibate during his long service in Kenya. I had a feeling that he was not going to be too heartbroken. In his last letter, a year or so ago, he told Norma that he'd bought a horse so that he could go riding with the colonel's daughter.

Chapter 31 – 1945

No doubt John would survive. So would Normal.

"Why don't we go out tonight, Fran," Norma said to me on her first night in town. "I hardly ever came up here during the air raids, so I'd like to see what's going on."

"We could go to the Overseas Club," I said, "but it's been quiet since the invasion; not nearly so much fun as it used to be. We could have a drink, though a soft one for me. There's always someone to dance with, if you'd like that."

"I'd love to dance. I haven't been dancing for ages."
"What about this latest boyfriend. What's he like," I asked.
"Andrew? Oh, you'll have to meet him. He's gorgeous, but he's not keen on dancing. Anyway he rarely comes to Wembley. The last time was Christmas. It's a lonely life."

"I can't imagine you being lonely for long, Norma. Are you thinking of marriage with this Andrew?"
"I hope so, as soon as John and I can get a divorce, and I hope that will be soon."
"I wonder what John will do?" "I wish you'd had a talk with him, instead of leaving it to your father. We won't get much information out of him."
"I couldn't face him, Frances. It's been far too long and he's made very little effort to keep in contact in recent years. He's a stranger to me now. I have nothing to say to him. That's the war, honey. It's happened to so many."
"Yes, we'll never bring back the old days. We've all changed. Our world has changed. Couples who can make a

go of it after a separation of six years are lucky. They would need to have had a good stable relationship before they had to part. Even then, it can't be easy. I hope Jack won't have to go to the Far East."

Shortly after we arrived at the club, Lyn came in with the striking looking fair-haired flight lieutenant she'd been going out with recently. They sat down with us and my friend Norma came sparkling to life. Norma was a beautiful girl with clouds of lovely black hair. She always attracted the men, but I didn't want anything to go wrong for Lyn this time.

"Keep your eyes off Robert," I said laughing. "Lyn is very keen."

"It takes two to tango, Frances. Stop worrying and have another lemonade."

I found myself wishing it was time to go home.

Lyn and Robert came back, and he asked Norma to dance.

"Where did she spring from?" Lyn said.

"We were at school together," I said. "She lives with her father in Wembley, but she's staying with me for a week or two because her husband is coming home from Africa and she doesn't want to see him. Actually, you met her once before. When we were at the Goldsmith Club she came to supper once."

"Can't say I remember. It's too long ago. I suppose I've had Rob after this."

"Not at all," I said. "You can turn on the charm. I'll kill you if you give in. He chose you in the first place, so it's up to you to keep him now."

It turned into an interesting evening. For a start, Lyn was the better dancer, and now she moved over to Robert and drew him on to the dance floor, while the band played 'A nightingale sang in Berkeley Square'. I saw one arm go round his neck, and then the other. He was getting her full attention. Was she reminding him of last night? How would I know, but she was playing a star role and he liked it.

Norma had already turned her attention to someone else. She was like a child let out of school, but at eleven o'clock I told her I was going home and, to my surprise, she came like a lamb. She'd had her fun.

"I enjoyed tonight, Frances," she said. "I felt I was sixteen again."

"Yes, you were a precocious sixteen-year-old" I said.

A Nightingale Sang

Chapter 32

1945

On the morning news bulletin we heard that the Americans had captured Leipzig. It brought back the sad memory of Du Bois' death and I wondered whether those many airmen had been buried in Leipzig. My thoughts went out to his young wife again and I wished her well.

I wonder how many young men died taking the city, or capturing Nuremberg the following day. We heard that seventeen thousand German troops had surrendered there.

The Soviets were still bombarding Berlin and, before the end of April they were occupying some northern and eastern suburbs. The city was under siege and surely even Hitler must know now that the end is near. Still his troops were putting up a powerful resistance. There was a terrible battle for Berlin.

Later that day Lyn rang.
"How is the love affaire going?"
"Really well," she said. "That's why I'm ringing. Rob and I have decided to get married."
"That's great news Lyn. I'm so happy for you. You knew him before the war, didn't you?

"Yes, he lived only a couple of miles from us at home. I've told you about my ex-fiancé from those days, Peter Holt, haven't I? Robert is actually Peter's cousin, so I'm keeping it in the family."

"That's a neat trick. Why haven't we met him before?"

"Oh, he's been abroad almost since the beginning of the war. He's only been back a few months. I met him in our local the last time I was at home and we appeared to be getting on very well, but I was really worried when we met your friend. Has she gone home?

"Yes, she went back when she knew that her father had explained the situation to John, her husband. On no account did she want him back. He's been away too long, Lyn. Apparently he wasn't too surprised. She says she intends to marry her present man as soon as she can get a divorce."

"My real reason for ringing is to ask you if you'll be my bridesmaid – matron-of-honour or whatever they call married ladies."

"I'll be matron-of-honoured, I'm sure. Are you getting married in church?"

"Oh, yes, C of E. You know I've been one of the stalwarts of the City Temple throughout the war."

"Yes, that marvellous man Donald Soper. I always enjoyed his visits to the club when we were there, but I remember how horrified you were when he said he would be prepared to hear confessions if anyone thought it would give them peace of mind."

"Lord yes. I wouldn't have that, but that's when I became one of his parishioners. He's a very special person. Anyway, thank you honey. Will you wear your wedding outfit? Sorry to sound mean, but I'm saving coupons. I could get something that goes with the colour."

"I would if I could, Lyn, but this baby is expanding my waistline."

"Can't say I've noticed."

"Don't worry, I have coupons at the moment and I'll be needing bigger clothes anyway, so we could go shopping together, couldn't we?"

"Sure. It will be a Mayday wedding. I hope the weather's fine. How about Saturday next for shopping? There's so little time, but Rob will be going away again. Don't know where to this time. We could try Harrods, O.K?"

"That suits me. I'll look forward to it. And, once again, I'm delighted for you."

So, at last, a happy ending for my friend. This is bound to be a bumper year for weddings, now that the men are starting to come home. Then we'll have a baby boom. We've waited a long time for this and now, you could say, life is getting back to normal, but to those of us who were at school six years ago, it's a life we don't know much about. We have a lot to learn.

The Americans are putting pressure on Britain to speed up the process of decolonisation, but very little, if anything, will be done while Winston Churchill is in power. There will be an election after the war, the first since the thirties and a first opportunity to vote for a great many of us.

For us, on the 1st May, the war was forgotten when we made our way to the City Temple, and later to the Savoy Hotel to celebrate our friend's marriage to Robert Holt. It was a happy day and they had all our good wishes when we saw them off to Scotland where Rob was to spend the rest of the war.

Lyn had not always been lucky in love so I was particularly happy to see how well she and Rob got along together. After demobilisation they would return to their native Kent, the Garden of England. "You should grow where you're planted, Rob said and, whether we agreed or not, that was his philosophy. It was a pretty place, their home town, and maybe they would be able to re-establish the splendid fruit farm which had been the pride and joy of Rob's family before the war. Failure to maintain it during the war years had been the death of his father.

"We have to celebrate the fall of Berlin," Cynthia said to me in the evening and, that night, I danced and sang in the Overseas Club for the last time. I would remember many a happy evening there.

Chapter 33

1945

On the morning of the 5th May, I had a cable from Jack 'Sans Origine'. The words were those of the War Office. The sentiments would have been expressed by millions of servicemen of all ranks over the war years:

Are you alright?
You are more than ever in my thoughts at this time.
Fondest love darling.

There was never any indication of where these cables came from, but John was obviously wondering whether his baby had been born. We all longed for a letter, but they were like gold dust, subject to the mercy of the waves.

Before long we were to hear that General Montgomery had received the surrender of the German forces:

"Five very dejected men had signed the surrender terms with an ordinary school pen, on a trestle table covered with an army blanket," Montgomery said.

This momentous news did not reach us at home until the six o'clock news on the evening of the 7th May. That was when we heard that the most destructive conflict the world had ever known would end at midnight, for us in Europe.

I was trying to write to Jack, wondering where he was and when I was likely to see him again, when I heard noises outside. My door opened suddenly. My brother and cousin had turned up out of the blue.

"There's no transport this evening. We're all going to walk to Buckingham Palace," somebody said. "Hurry up, everybody will be there."

"Come in for a few minutes," I said. Since late afternoon I had been ignoring the niggling pains in my stomach, but now it was time to admit that I would not be going to Buckingham Palace.

"I'm afraid it's an ambulance I need," I said.

My landlady was a doctor and I knew she wouldn't mind waiting with me. "Don't let me delay you," I said. "The whole country will be there."

Rachel came in minutes and was kindness itself. "Frances will be alright," she said. "I'll stay until the ambulance arrives. Off you go and enjoy yourselves."

My brother looked worried. With only a year between us, we had always been the best of friends. Rachel was fond of him too.

"Don't worry Patrick. We'll be fine here."

We seemed to be waiting ages. "I bet those ambulance men are celebrating," I said, and the last minutes of wartime Europe were ticking away as our doorbell rang and midnight chimed from the town hall clock. I climbed into the back of the ambulance, followed by one of the men. It was an exciting time and, as we clanged our way down the street, every church bell in the country rang out to celebrate the peace. Apparently, it had been decided not to sound a last 'All Clear' because of its unhappy associations.

Every door in London was open that night; every window was blazing with light. No more black-out. How I hated that black-out. The streets were crowded with people hugging and kissing each other, all reserve abandoned.

The ambulance man encouraged me to watch the happy crowds who thronged the streets. We were at the hospital in no time, but the noise went on. The staff and, I suppose, anyone who cared to join in, were in the grounds singing and cheering.

"Ah, our first Victory baby," the nurse said as I walked up the corridor.

That happy statement was bit premature. My life of dancing and gymnastics had produced muscles that were not likely to give way in a hurry. At three o'clock the following afternoon, she put her head around the door. "Do you want to hear Mr. Churchill?" she asked. I gave her what I hoped was a perishing look.

"No, but I want you," I said.

She came in a hurry and, between us we produced a beautiful baby girl.

Chapter 34

1945

It was very hot in London the day we went to the polls in July 1945. The fine weather meant that everyone who could, turned out, and everyone looked happy. There was a long delay waiting for the results because all the servicemen had an opportunity to vote wherever in the world they happened to be.

A massive shock awaited the Tories. It was a landslide victory for Labour. They won about four hundred seats, twice as many as their Conservative opponents. That Winston Churchill, the revered leader of the war years, should have been toppled from power, would have been unthinkable a year before.

Young people supported the Left. It was said that about ninety per cent of Air Force personnel, the youngest and least conservative of the fighting forces, voted Labour.

Apart from improvements in social services, Labour would begin the gradual dissolution of the British Empire. Empire day was dropped as a school holiday.

The changes were inevitable. People who remembered the hungry years; the General Strike of 1926, the Jarrow-on-Tyne hunger marchers, the Welsh mining community and the unemployed of the Scottish industrial belt, would no longer tolerate less than a fair chance to improve their lot. They had fought for a better world for everyone and that was what they intended to get.

That was the general feeling at the end of the war.

Unexpectedly there was a telephone call from Jack.

"I'm in Sheerness," he said.

"For heaven's sake, what are you doing there?"

"We're just back from Rotterdam, and we leave in the morning for Norway."

"Oh no, does that mean I'm not going to see you?"

"That's why I'm ringing. I have the evening off and I'm going to try and get to London for a couple of hours. It's the best I can do. It'll be hello and goodbye, I'm afraid, but I've got to see you and my new daughter. The train leaves in ten minutes, so I'll be with you soon. Bye darling."

By my reckoning he would arrive around seven or so. It was the best news I could have had. The baby was looking like a rosebud in her best pink. Fortunately I had got my rations earlier in the day so I had some meat to make a casserole with plenty of vegetables. Servicemen hated taking food from civilians because they were so much better fed than we were, but I knew Jack wouldn't want to waste time going out. He wouldn't be able to resist the food.

Chapter 34 – 1945

I was in a state of nervous tension by the time Jack arrived, but seeing him looking well and suntanned and handsome, was worth all the waiting. He stood and looked at the baby for a long time. I knew he'd have been expecting a big smile and a head of curls. There wasn't much chance to see new born babies at sea.

"She's very small," he said. "Will she be alright?"

"Oh sit down and have your meal," I said. "The baby is fine and she's quite the most beautiful child I've ever seen. She sleeps most of the time. That's how they grow, so you don't have to worry."

"I know you're right. I just thought she'd be bigger."

I give up.

"By the way, you look great," he said. "Having a baby hasn't done you any harm."
"Where were you on VE-Day?" I said. "I was thinking about you in the midst of my turmoil."

"We were half-way across the ocean. It was the last Atlantic convoy of the war. We celebrated, of course, but I broke my arm. We had an obstacle race and I fell twenty feet through what was supposed to be a safety net. The captain scrawled across the deck, 'NELSON HELL! THIS IS WHERE CONWAY FELL'.

"It was strapped up until we got to St. Johns. They wanted to keep me there. I wasn't having that and I told them I had information about certain weapons needed in the Far East, so I had to get back. That didn't impress them, I'm afraid, so I enlisted the help of the captain. He came ashore and got me out of that place. I'd have languished away there. There isn't even a decent pub in St. John's."

I told him he always got his priorities right.

"Come here," he said. "My God, I've been waiting for this," undoing a few buttons.
"Good job that innocent baby is asleep," I said.

An hour later I woke John and called a taxi. "What were you doing in Rotterdam?" I asked.

"We were on a courtesy call," he said. "It's in a desperate state. There's hardly a stone left on a stone and they're starving. Every member of the crew went ashore laden with chocolates and cigarettes and any other luxury they could lay their hands on. It's terrible to see a proud people reduced to that. Back on the ship, a crowd gathered on the quayside and everything edible was lobbed overboard. Bread was badly needed. No one wanted anything in return, but they pressed watches and fountain pens and things on us. It was essential for their self-respect that they should do that, I suppose."
"My God, I hope there'll never be another war. It's obscene," I said.

Chapter 34 – 1945

"We left Rotterdam on Tuesday afternoon, but four or five miles down the Rhine, we discovered we had five stowaways on board – young lads, anxious to get to England. It was awful to have to take them back."

"What will you be doing in Norway?" I asked.

"We'll be calling at every port from Bergen north to Tromso. Then south again to Kristiansand to escort the liner which will be taking the German prisoners-of-war back to Bremerhaven. After that, it'll be back to Blighty for twenty-eight days leave. Oh boy, am I looking forward to that. Will you go to Westport?"

"I've got a sailing ticket for the 3rd August, so I'll be there whenever you get that leave. It will be wonderful. I wish you could spend the night."

"It won't be long now," he said. "The Japanese can't hold out much longer, surely. Tokyo's being pounded. I'll see you in Westport."

"Don't be too sympathetic with those Nordics," I said, "those collaboratoresses."

"Oh, you've heard about them, have you?" he said. "You haven't a thing to worry about. They're not a patch on my colleen."

I had a long sad ride back to Chelsea.

After Jack left, I longed to get out of London. The raids, the black-outs, the food – that awful wartime food had all taken their toll. I was longing to go home. Nothing and nowhere equalled the comfort of Rosbeg at that time, and Jack loved it as much as I did. There was nothing I wanted more now than to see them all again even though it meant that tedious journey once more. I would endure it gladly.

I sent the pram to Euston in advance and my brother came to help me with the baby in the morning.

Chapter 35

1945

The Battle of the Atlantic is over now, but this story couldn't end without a word of praise for the brave men who sailed Ireland's wartime merchant fleet to carry essential commodities back home.

At the beginning of the war, the Irish fleet sailed in convoy with British ships, but from early 1942 they sailed alone, protected only by the green, white and orange flag or neutral Eire painted on their hulls. Their courage was largely unacknowledged, even in their own country.

When the Limerick Steamship Company's ship *Clonlara* was torpedoed in the Atlantic in August 1941, with the loss of most of her crew, the report in the papers took second place to the fact that rain had marred the opening of the local horse show. Only three days earlier, *Clonlara* had rescued the thirteen survivors of a British ship. They were thirteen of over five hundred survivors rescued by the small Irish merchant fleet during the war years.

All seven Irish-owned tankers were sunk during the first three years of the war.

Irish Shipping Limited, which was formed in 1941, lost two of their ships, 'Irish Pine' and 'Irish Oak'. They were two of the forty ships flying the Irish tricolour which were attacked and sunk or damaged between February 1940 and May 1945. The loss of *The City of Waterford* is, perhaps, the most dramatic story of them all.

In September 1941, '*City of Waterford*' joined a British convoy at Milford Haven. It was a large convoy escorted by an aircraft carrier, a destroyer, six corvettes, two other naval ships and, most importantly, a hospital ship. The convoy was attacked and 'City of Waterford' was holed below the waterline. Her crew of twenty-three men was forced to abandon ship and they pulled away in two life boats. They were picked up by a naval sloop and transferred to the hospital ship, *Walmer Castle*.

Later that night, the convoy was attacked and three ships were lost. Their crews, too, were picked up by *Walmer Castle* and the *City of Waterford* crewmen helped with the rescue of the blinded, burned or badly wounded survivors.

At dawn, the overcrowded hospital ship was attacked by a German plane and set on fire and most of those who could were forced to abandon the stricken ship. Thirteen men stayed aboard, including the *City of Waterford*'s captain and her engineer, James Ryan, who helped to dump shells and other combustible material.

Walmer Castle went to the bottom in the afternoon with several of the Irish crewmen, including the captain. Three more ships and fifty-five men were lost during the following night, but the survivors reached Gibraltar and were carried back to Liverpool aboard the B & I ship *Leinster*, to be greeted by the sound of German bombers attacking that important port.

When the European war ended in May 1945, de Valera did express the nation's gratitude to the brave men of our merchant fleet.

A Nightingale Sang

Chapter 36

1945

There was a very pleasant surprise for me in Westport. Nan, my very first friend and the girl who had travelled with me to London the day war was declared, was visiting her parents. They were our neighbours in Rosbeg. She and I had travelled to London together the night before war was declared. She joined the WAAF, the Women's Air Force, and had married a squadron leader, and now here she was with her year-old daughter.

"Nan," I said, when I had greeted my mother and father, "this is the nicest thing that could have happened."

"I know. I only arrived yesterday and I couldn't believe it when they said you were coming. This is Eigan."

"She's gorgeous," I said. She was a beautiful child with big brown eyes and dark brown curls. "I can't show you my little beauty because the girls have run away with the carry cot. I won't get a chance to hold her now, unless she gets cross, of course. I bet she'll be given back then. I'd like to think that there'll be a well-worn track between our houses when these children are older."

"Indeed, I hope so," she replied. "It's absolute heaven here. I don't know how we were ever able to leave it. How long are you staying?"

"Well, Jack will be getting twenty-eight days leave as soon as the war ends, so everything depends on how long

Japan can hold out and where he will be going afterwards. How long do you intend to stay?"

"We'll be here for Harold's after-the-war leave anyway and that's not bad, is it?"

I'd been home only a few days when the terrible news of the total destruction of the Japanese city of Hiroshima filled the newspapers and, three days later, on the 9th August, the annihilation of Nagasaki, by this new and fearful atomic bomb.

At school we had learnt of mens' attempts to split the atom. It meant nothing then, but now we have the shocking evidence of their success, and two names will forever be synonymous with the awful reality of the depths to which mans' inhumanity can sink.

Within days, surrender was forced on the Japanese and, on the 15th August 1945, I have to say that all condemnation was set aside in the relief of knowing that the war was over at last and we were going to celebrate.

Women were not to be seen drinking in public in the West of Ireland at that time, but Nan and I decided that this was as good a time as any to show the men that we, too, could share their favourite pastime.

Mind you, our local was not the height of luxury. The seats were likely to be sacks of meal, and sides of bacon decorated the offside of the bar. The owner of this tavern was a large blonde lady who had spent her most productive years in America – a returned Yank, in fact. She was a lovely good-natured lady for whom I had a lot of affection. She was amused when I told her we were there, not for a few rashers or a bag of flour, but to celebrate the outbreak of peace in the world. and to accustom the local men to the sight of women sharing their favourite pastime.

"And we don't want to be hidden away beside the blacked-out range in the back kitchen," I said. "We want our refreshment here at the bar."

She thought that would be too much of a shock for the sensibilities of the local males. "Sure there'd be nothing for ye to sit on anyway," she said. She had spent forty years in New York, but she'd never 'lost the brogue', and that was considered a compliment in our part of the world. "I'll put ye in the snug," she said.

It was there, behind a smelly green curtain that had seen better days, that Nan and I drank to the end of the Second World War. We drank in silence for fear of upsetting the customers in the bar, and that wasn't an easy thing to do. We were alone and lonely, but when we got home, there was a message from our old friends, Grace and Arthur, to say that they were giving a party and they would expect us during the evening. It was good news and there was plenty of music and gaiety for us before sunrise on the 16th August.

As soon as the war was over; Jack got his long leave. He hitched a trip on a destroyer sailing to Moville in Donegal, but any hope of avoiding customs duty was dashed when he was instructed to travel back across the Border to Derry before proceeding to Éire.

His arrival caused endless excitement and when he produced presents for the younger members of the family, he was a very popular visitor.

"What did you do in Norway?" I wanted to know, when all the excitement died down.

"From Bergen, our first port of call, we sailed to the most northerly port of Tromso. The Norwegian fiords are beautiful and we hardly ever saw the open sea. We were above the Arctic Circle when we visited Harstad in the Lofoten Islands and the lads were able to play football there at two o'clock in the morning by the light of the midnight sun. Afterwards, we were entertained by the 6th Airborne Division and were invited to help ourselves to the best of the liqueurs left behind by the departing Germans.

"From Harstad we sailed south to Kristiansand to escort the German prisoners-of-war home."
"How were the Germans after their defeat?" I asked.
"We provided a token guard aboard their ship and we found them friendly and co-operative, but contemptuous of Norway's efforts to defend the country."
"In Bremerhaven, we found the Germans on the point of starvation," Jack continued.
"Yes, I have friends in England who have already formed committees for the collection and distribution of food

and other shortages in Germany," I said, "but it's a drop in the ocean of their suffering."

It was wonderful to have Jack home for a whole month. The weather was good and we were able to enjoy sailing and fishing trips, as well as picnicking on the islands. We were both anxious to visit Inisheeny again, for old time's sake and on that particular day we gave all would-be passengers the slip by leaving on the tide at seven o'clock in the morning. It was one of the best days of the holiday and we ended it by dancing in our local 'ballroom of romance'.

It would have been impossible not to enjoy these lovely care free summer days in our favourite place in the world.

We cycled and walked, danced, drank and climbed mountains, and enjoyed the company of some of our favourite people. It was a summer to remember for the rest of our lives. We were young and in love, and at the beginning of a marriage that was full of promise and, above all, the war which had marred our young lives was over.

Nevertheless, I found it impossible not to go over the past six years in thought: To remember my cousin, George Balmforth, my lovely friend Willy Palmer, a volunteer for a suicide mission; the two Simmons boys, Cecil Anderson, Jim Hennessy, Toby Duncan and so many more. Rosbeg would be the poorer for their loss. We would not forget.

Sadly too we would remember with gratitude the happy, confident young men of the Air Force who gave their lives over London that we might live. There was so much to remind us of the futility of war, but beyond that we are proud to remember the splendid young men who never lost their youthful sense of humour even when there was little hope of them seeing the morning.

Pray that it will never happen again.

Epilogue

All this was a long time ago, and I'm looking back across a life that has been a love song. From parents and siblings, to friends and lovers, to children and grandchildren and especially to the man who stood beside me in that sad grey church when we were young and the world was upside down. I have loved them all.

Half a century would pass before we had the party we had promised ourselves at the height of the war, before Jack would hold my hand and sing:

> *For you are beautiful*
> *And I have loved you dearly,*
> *More dearly than the spoken word can tell*

It hasn't been all sunshine, but in the dark corners when I am frightened or lonely, or looking anxiously over a world full of pitfalls for children who were thousands of miles away, my faith was there, warm and comforting; a permanent source of light.

There was the time I almost lost Jack in a near fatal illness. That was the time he told our long-time friend Grace that he couldn't die because I was waiting, suntanned after a day on the bay. "She came walking towards me when I was nearly gone," he said, "and I had to come back."

However long there is to go now, I know the love song will last to the end – and beyond.

.

Strange to look back
to remember
the people I knew
for a short space of time
long ago

Years at school
years at war
married years
child-bearing, child rearing,
forgetting the people I'd met in the past
with so much to do
so many to care for

But now I remember
the soft black nights
dancing, singing, laughing, loving,
forgetting the bombers, in your arms.

.

A Nightingale Sang